M & E

M & E Handbooks ɪ _____ ....ᴜᴇᴅ reading for examination syllabuses all over the world. Because each Handbook covers its subject clearly and concisely, books in the series form a vital part of many college, university, school and home study courses.

Handbooks contain detailed information stripped of unnecessary padding, making each title a comprehensive self-tuition course. They are amplified with numerous self-testing questions in the form of Progress Tests at the end of each chapter, each text-referenced for easy checking. Every Handbook closes with an appendix which advises on examination technique. For all these reasons, Handbooks are ideal for pre-examination revision.

The handy pocket-book size and competitive price make Handbooks the perfect choice for anyone who wants to grasp the essentials of a subject quickly and easily.

THE M & E HANDBOOK SERIES

Elements of Finance for Managers

B K R Watts, BA, AMBIM

Pitman Publishing Limited
128 Long Acre, London WC2E 9AN

A Longman Group Company

First published 1976
Reprinted 1977
Reprinted 1979
Reprinted 1986

© Pitman Publishing Ltd 1976

ISBN 0 7121 0551 4

Typeset, printed and bound in Great Britain
by Richard Clay (The Chaucer Press) Ltd,
Bungay, Suffolk

PREFACE

THIS book is intended to give an insight into finance to professional, scientific, technical and general managers and staff who may have no previous grounding in finance or accountancy. It will be of value to the general reader who wants to improve his appreciation of company financial affairs, and to the increasing number of managers undertaking management courses, in particular those of the Institute of Works Managers, the postgraduate Diploma in Management Studies, National Examinations Board in Supervisory Studies' Diploma in Administrative Management, the Diploma in Marketing, the many in-company courses and courses organised by Training Boards, and in addition, to students on first-year business study degree courses, and those for Higher National Certificate, Chartered Institute of Transport and Institute of Chartered Secretaries and Administrators' examinations.

Managers clearly need a sound grasp of finance if they are to make effective use of the resources entrusted to them. The impact of inflation and the consequent need for closer financial control emphasise the need for a surer appreciation of available financial techniques in areas of planning and controlling resources. Specialist managers and staff can no longer leave the appreciation of financial aspects to others; they must become more involved in the financial implications of their specialist decisions.

This book is not intended to be an exhaustive text book; it does, however, cover the essentials of finance. It is written in a straightforward manner with the minimum use of the jargon and complex terminology that is characteristic of accountancy and finance, and where its use is necessary, definitions are given either in the text or in the Glossary. Furthermore, a considerable number of examples illustrate principles, and problems posed within the text, to consolidate and test the reader's understanding at each important stage in the development of the subject.

The student is advised to read quickly through the chapter and section headings and the numbered paragraph headings to get an overall picture of the contents. Then he should read through each section in sequence. The Progress Tests at the end of each chapter are for self-examination and revision.

The objective is that the reader should acquire a basic knowledge of finance which he may develop by further reading, or by attending courses to improve his own effectiveness in financial matters, to the improvement of both his own and his company's performance.

October 1975   B.K.R.W.

CONTENTS

LIST OF ILLUSTRATIONS

LIST OF TABLES

PART ONE

MONEY: WHERE DOES IT COME FROM AND HOW DO WE RECORD IT?

CHAPTER I

MONEY: WHERE DOES IT COME FROM?

THE ORIGINS OF MONEY

1. Barter. In all probability earliest man was self-sufficient, providing all his own food, shelter, clothing and weapons. However, although primitive, a system of specialisation surely developed when individuals noticed that they possessed special talents; somebody with a flair for making stone weapons and tools would exchange them for food supplied by others who were better at hunting. Others more adept at making clothes would swap these for tools and food. Thus individuals tended to specialise in the production of goods in which they had a relative advantage, and obtained other goods by exchange or barter.

In fact, barter is still widely used today, particularly in trade between the Eastern countries and Europe, and one remembers with interest the tasty offer from a Middle East State to buy a VC 10 for £3 million worth of apples.

2. Disadvantages of barter. However, the system of barter contains inherent disadvantages that handicap the development of specialisation and exchange. These disadvantages are:

(*a*) The need for a double coincidence of wants before exchange can take place. In other words, the Cornish tin miner desiring purple cloth had first to find a Phoenician trader who wanted tin.

1

(*b*) Secondly, there is a problem of setting the rate of exchange between goods, *e.g.* cloth and tin.

(*c*) As a result, certain goods may become very expensive in terms of others. Perhaps a Phoenician trader was not prepared to accept excessive amounts of tin for his valuable cloth.

(*d*) Certain goods are imperfectly divisible, *e.g.* perhaps a herdsman was not willing to exchange part of a sheep for vegetables. Consequently, traders turned their attention to indirect exchange which overcame the disadvantages of barter. By means of a medium of exchange, *i.e.* money, trader A can sell his goods to trader B for money with which A can buy goods of his choice.

3. Functions of money. Money is anything that is widely accepted as a medium of exchange. Its functions are summarised as:

(*a*) *A medium of exchange*. A variety of goods have been successfully used as money. Salt, tobacco, sugar, flour, cattle, women, dried cod and metals have been generally acceptable at one time or another.

(*b*) *A measure of value*. Money acts as a common denominator or a unit of account by which relative values or prices of all goods can be compared.

(*c*) *A store of value*. Money possesses lasting qualities enabling its owner to postpone purchasing power.

(*d*) *A standard of deferred payment*. It is a measuring unit of debt and permits future settlement of debt.

4. Qualities of money. Metals quickly replaced other media of exchange. Paper in turn superseded metal in the twentieth century; both possess clear advantages over other forms of money. These advantages are:

(*a*) Generally acceptable as a *medium of exchange*.

(*b*) *Portability*.

(*c*) *Recognisability*.

(*d*) *Divisibility*.

(*e*) *Durability*—paper is clearly less durable than metal money.

(*f*) *Scarcity*.

(*g*) *Stability of value*. The recent history of the pound has been disappointing in this respect; the depreciating value of sterling is due in the main to the failure of the authorities to control the supply of money.

5. Summary of types of money. Legal tender is money that is legally enforceable in settlement of debts. However, in practice there are numerous forms of money that are generally acceptable in that they fulfil one or more of the functions outlined in 3. Money in this general sense takes the following forms:

(*a*) *Precious metal*, in particular gold and silver.

(*b*) *Coins.*

(*c*) *Bank notes.*

(*d*) *Bank deposits.* These are transferred by cheques.

(*e*) *Bills of exchange.* These are negotiable instruments. Traders are prepared to accept a bill in settlement of a debt.

(*f*) *Treasury bills.* These are ninety-one day promissory notes, dating from 1877, by which the State borrows money to overcome irregularities in Government taxation revenue. Since they are repayable in full at maturity, they are free of risk and therefore acceptable in settlement of debts.

(*g*) *Trade credit.* Inter-company debts arising through trade credit may cancel out each other. Thus settlement is made without recourse to cheques or cash payments.

EVOLUTION OF BANKING

6. Growth of trade. With the development of trade in the late Middle Ages, brought about by improvements in communication and transport systems, there were increasing demands for banking facilities. The growth in national and international trade meant:

(*a*) *There were shortages of cash.* Merchants and businessmen buying or producing in anticipation of future demand needed to borrow money.

(*b*) *Traders needed a means of facilitating exchanges.* Bills of exchange and other negotiable instruments were devised as convenient means of aiding exchanges. They economised in the use of cash and were readily acceptable by traders in settlement of debts. Furthermore, they provided additional security since cash need not change hands.

7. Money-lenders and goldsmiths. Money-lenders and gold-smiths were the fore-runners of the present commercial banks. The growth of trade created affluence for an increasing number of traders and businessmen who desired safe-keeping of their wealth. The vaults and strong-rooms of goldsmiths were the obvious places for the depositing of liquid funds which were repayable on presentation of the receipt. In return, bank deposit receipts were issued. The main developments were as follows:

(a) Deposit receipts that acknowledged the existence of a corresponding sum at the bank were themselves acceptable consideration for settlement of debts and circulated as early forms of *bank notes*.

(b) These early bankers noticed that they were perma-nently holding cash and were therefore encouraged to issue deposit receipts in excess of actual holdings of cash. Thus *bank credit* was created.

(c) Money-lenders and goldsmiths spread their range of banking services by acting as intermediaries, placing people with idle funds for *investment* with merchants who desired loans.

8. Commercial banks and the Bank of England. The com-mercial banks—the most important being Lloyds, National Westminster, Midland and Barclays—have gained their present prominent position as a result of mergers and takeovers over the past two hundred years.

The Bank of England dates back to 1694. Its position was strengthened by the *Bank Charter Act* 1844 which prevented new banks from issuing bank notes, and gradually extinguished the rights of existing banks in this respect, so that today the Bank has a monopoly of note issue in England.

By the twentieth century it was responsible for carrying out government monetary policy, and in 1946 nationalisation gave it powers over the commercial banks.

9. Creation of bank credit. So far this chapter has served to introduce the reader to money and banking. Indeed its brevity implies a prior knowledge of the subject matter. However, this section is particularly important for the manager wishing to understand the intricacies of the financial system, since creation of credit lies at the very heart of the subject. Further-more, a sound grasp of the system is essential at the outset if one is to have an appreciation of government monetary policy, of inflation and, in more practical terms, of how the bank manager is likely to respond to a request for overdraft facilities.

Imagine that a customer X deposits £1,000 in cash at a bank and receives a cheque book. The transaction will affect the bank's Balance Sheet as follows:

BANK'S BALANCE SHEET

Liabilities		Assets	
X Bank deposit	£1,000	Cash	£1,000

If banking experience is such that customers generally demand only 10 per cent of deposits in cash and all other transactions are carried out by cheque, then the bank may safely lend part of this initial deposit to other customers. Thus the bank may advance Y £900 (90 per cent of £1,000); the Balance Sheet now looks like this:

BANK'S BALANCE SHEET

X Bank deposit	£1,000	Cash	£1,000
Y Bank deposit	900	Advance to Y	900
	£1,900		£1,900

But Y will demand only 10 per cent of his deposit in cash, and all other transactions are completed by cheque. Therefore Z may receive an advance of 90 per cent of Y's deposit so that the Balance Sheet is now as follows:

BANK'S BALANCE SHEET

X Bank deposit	£1,000	Cash	£1,000
Y Bank deposit	900	Advance to Y	900
Z Bank deposit	810	Advance to Z	810
	£2,710		£2,710

Similarly the bank can create additional credit as follows:

90% of £810
90% of 90% of £810
90% of 90% of 90% of £810, etc.

Eventually the Balance Sheet will look like this:

BANK'S BALANCE SHEET

Total deposits	£10,000	Cash	£1,000
		Total advances	9,000
	£10,000		£10,000

Total deposits amount to £10,000; if these customers demand 10 per cent of these deposits in cash then the bank is safely able to accommodate them since it holds total cash of £1,000. Thus this bank has created credit or additional purchasing power for customers of £9,000 because it knows that its customers will require only marginal amounts of their deposits in cash at any one time.

10. The banks' objectives. Clearing banks are public companies whose objectives appear to be:

(a) *Profitability of operations* for the benefit of shareholders.

(b) *Security of depositors' funds.*

(c) *Liquidity of assets* to enable banks to pay on demand.

Liquidity describes the ease and speed with which an asset can be converted into cash.

The third objective demands that banks maintain an adequate proportion of depositors' funds in cash or near-money (liquid assets) which can be encashed without delay should a run on the bank occur. The measure of liquid assets as a percentage of total deposits is the liquidity ratio.

11. Example of the reserve ratio (liquidity ratio). There follows as an example a diary of events with related liquidity ratios for the Smiths Bank, Lincoln drawn from the *National Westminster Bank Review* February 1972.

Date	Event	Price of wheat	liquidity ratio %
1845	Fairly good wheat harvest	45s. 1d.	17
1846	Wheat in short supply in England and Europe	94s. 10d.	25·4
1847	Poor harvest, improving imports		23·2
1853	Poor harvest, few imports	80s. and over	54·4
1854	,, ,, ,, ,,	80s. and over	53·2
1855	,, ,, ,, ,,	80s. and over	51·2
1856	Fair harvest	70s. and over	40·1
1857	Good harvest		29·9
1857–72	Settled conditions		x̄ 28·71
1872	Several bankruptcies: The Bank suffers losses one of £59,000		
1875	Examination of whole of Bank's asset structure		
1873–91	Settled conditions		x̄ 29·92

NOTE: x̄ is the arithmetic mean (average).

These events illustrate that at this Bank, and presumably at others as well, there was initially no conscious attempt to regulate the liquidity ratio; it was rather a function of public demand and customers' deposits, which depended on the state of local agriculture and industry. The high liquidity ratio coincides with high prices of wheat, and may be explained by the fact that farmers who would be the Bank's chief customers and who would consequently be fairly affluent at these times, would be depositing substantial sums of cash. Over the settled period 1857–72 the average liquidity ratio (x̄) was 28·71 per cent with a standard deviation of 4·9. Thus the liquidity ratio fluctuated considerably around this average figure. The substantial losses in 1872 caused a flurry of activity and from the discussion and analysis that followed a new policy emerged. The Bank would immediately cut back on long-term loans and would in future hold extra amounts of liquid government securities as insurance.

In 1875 after further re-examination of banking policy, this Bank made a decision to regulate the ratio in the future at a stable and prudent (and profitable) level. "It is considered by experienced men of business that a bank ought to hold in available funds to the extent of $\frac{1}{3}$ of its liabilities" (deposits). The impact of this new policy is evidenced by the higher average liquidity ratio over the period 1875–91 of 29·9 per cent, and the lower standard deviation of 3·0. In other words, the liquid reserves were now higher and consciously maintained at this level.

12. Banks and monetary policy. The level of economic activity and employment is determined by the level of total spending by consumers, government, business and foreigners who buy British goods. If this expenditure is excessive in relation to productive capacity, then inflation results; if it is deficient then unemployment results. Consequently, the government must keep a close watch on total expenditure to ensure that economic activity is consistent with its objectives; reflating if it falls too low and deflating if too high. Monetary and fiscal policy are the main instruments for this economic policy.

Monetary policy is a general market weapon to regulate total demand, and works in the following two ways:

(*a*) Changes in interest rates affect investment decisions as follows:

(*i*) Higher rates of interest cause businessmen to defer decisions to buy new plant and equipment. Individuals tend to put off borrowing until rates are lower.
(*ii*) Businessmen making only very slim profit margins are forced to reduce stocks if they have to pay higher interest rates, say, on borrowed money financing these stocks.

(*b*) Banks are forced to cut back on advances to customers, particularly if the Treasury via the Bank of England restricts the supply of money in the monetary system.

(*i*) The Bank of England may demand that the banks deposit a proportion of their total deposits in cash with the Bank. Naturally this immediately reduces the banks' ability to advance loans but the eventual reduction in bank credit will be a multiple of the cash called in as explained in **9**.
(*ii*) The Bank may sell securities (bills of exchange) in the money market. If these sales are sufficiently large then the banks will have to call in advances to replenish their cash balances already depleted by their payments to the Bank as their customers' cheques are cleared.
(*iii*) The Bank may announce a change in its minimum lending rate as an indication of the anticipated rates of interest in the money markets.

13. Fiscal policy. This refers to the government's budgetary measures to regulate economic activity which may be classified as *easy* or *tight* budgets, *e.g.* 1959 and 1967 respectively. Both monetary and fiscal policy have a direct influence on economic activity and on the fortunes of individual companies. Managers are only too well aware of the impact of budgets, minimum lending rate and monetary policy and of the stop–go policies that have characterised the post-war period, but may not be too clear of the chain of events in the process.

Thus, assuming that the government wishes to reflate the economy either through an increase in government expenditure, investment, exports or consumer expenditure on consumer durables or capital goods, then the following events occur:

    (*a*) Extra employment in the capital goods industries.
    (*b*) Increased spending on consumer goods.
    (*c*) Extra employment in the consumer goods industries.
    (*d*) Hence still further spending on consumer goods.
    (*e*) Further increase in output of consumer goods. Thus the initial increase in expenditure has had a multiplier effect, swelling the level of total incomes, consumption and employment.
    (*f*) More capital goods are required eventually to satisfy the increase in demand, which in turn has a further multiplier effect on incomes, consumption and employment.

A deflationary policy has an opposite effect on profits, income, employment and economic activity generally.

In conclusion, many businessmen now realise that the fortunes of their companies do not rest solely on the managers' ability to compete successfully in the market-place; since the war, the government has played a more participative role in industry, checking and regulating it in order to secure predetermined economic, social and political objectives.

PROGRESS TEST 1

1. What do you understand by the word "money?" **(3–5)**
2. To what extent can banks create money? **(7–11)**

CHAPTER II

FINANCE FOR INDUSTRY

THE CAPITAL MARKET

1. The capital market. Generally speaking, savings (making money available for borrowers) and investment (the using of money for the purchase of capital goods and equipment) are undertaken by different parties, and some mechanism is needed to co-ordinate these forces of demand and supply. This is done by the capital market through its many different specialist institutions, which act as intermediaries and channel the savings of companies and individuals to borrowers. The main institutions are as follows:

    (*a*) Commercial banks.
    (*b*) Merchant banks.
    (*c*) Discount houses.
    (*d*) Insurance companies and pension funds.
    (*e*) Investment trusts, etc.
    (*f*) The Stock Exchange.

2. Categories of capital. In order to examine more closely the main sources of capital, and the roles of the financial institutions, it is convenient to classify these funds under broad headings. They may be grouped according to risk, *e.g.* low-, medium- and high-risk capital. However, it is more satisfactory to use liquidity as the criterion. In this way the institutions are members either of the money market or the capital market. The former provides industry, in the broadest sense, with very short-term loans. The latter is concerned with longer-term loans but will include some institutions which also operate in the money market, *e.g.* the commercial banks, whose advances contribute towards industry's working capital. The main categories of capital are as follows:

    (*a*) Long-term capital (*i.e.* share and loan capital).

(*b*) Short- and medium-term capital (*i.e.* working or circulating capital).

(*c*) Specialist finance.

THE NEW ISSUES MARKET

3. Advantages of private companies.

(*a*) Private companies are likely to be small enough to benefit from the following factors:

(*i*) Close contact between directors, staff and employees.

(*ii*) Greater flexibility.

(*iii*) The stimulus of members' self-interest.

(*b*) They possess the following privileges:

(*i*) Fewer documentary requirements compared with public companies.

(*ii*) Fewer procedural requirements.

(*c*) Control is exercised by members who can manage the company in their own interest, uninfluenced by public opinion; *i.e.* they are not in the public eye.

(*d*) They are *secure from take-over-bids*.

(*e*) They can discount current profitability for longer-term development, which would reduce the market valuation of public companies and invite take-over bids.

4. Advantages of public companies.

(*a*) Public companies may invite the general public to subscribe capital and thereby raise more money than by private subscription.

(*b*) They may secure the advantages of quotation (*see* 5).

(*c*) Their status lessens the impact of death duties on shareholders who may more readily sell shares to realise funds.

Generally, these advantages outweigh those for private companies; hence the tendency for conversion at some stage in the development of firms.

5. Reasons for share quotation. Every year about a hundred privately owned companies seek a Stock Exchange quotation for their shares for one or more of the following reasons:

(*a*) Shareholders of unquoted companies may request a *floatation* which, while adding nothing to the capital resources of the company, does provide them with cash or marketable shares which may be used for a variety of purposes such as the spread of investment risk.

(*b*) Capital commitments may outstretch net cash flow, in which case the new issues market may be the suitable source of new permanent capital or long-term loans. In addition, banks, a main source of working capital, may react more sympathetically to requests from quoted companies. On the other hand, companies wishing to reduce their dependence on bank finance, which may be withdrawn in times of severe credit squeeze, may be attracted towards the long-term finance of the new issues market.

(*c*) Quoted shares are readily marketable and acceptable and may be given as consideration in merger and take-over transactions.

(*d*) Quotation seems to invest companies with a superior status. This may be important to customers, who often like to know the trading patterns and financial resources of their suppliers.

(*e*) The market tends to place a higher valuation on quoted companies than private investors do, and this is naturally to the benefit of shareholders.

6. Loan stock quotations. A company wishing to raise additional capital may prefer to float an issue of loan stock. These securities, which offer the subscriber a fixed rate of interest, are repayable at a predetermined date and can be bought and sold in the stock market like shares.

7. Disadvantages of quotation. Against the above advantages must be set the following disadvantages:

(*a*) Quotation may be accomplished at a cost to some shareholders in the form of loss of control in the conduct of the business. However, it is not essential that equity should be made public, and it may be possible to raise capital by an issue of quoted loan stock instead of equity, so that equity and control is retained, as Ferranti, for example, has done in the past.

(*b*) The exacting Stock Exchange requirements place greater responsibilities on the board of directors. Quotation also demands a fair distribution policy and consistent profits. Failure on the part of directors will damage the company's public standing.

(*c*) The disclosure of information for shareholders reviewing progress (*e.g.* growth prospects and circumstances which might materially affect share prices), may be useful to competitors. However, the *Companies Act* 1967 partly overcomes this objection since all limited liability companies are required to publish trading and financial details.

(*d*) Going public is expensive.

(*e*) The company is vulnerable to take-over bids.

8. Types of issues. A company may make its securities available to investors by the following means:

(*a*) An issue by *prospectus*:

(*i*) A public issue by the company;
(*ii*) an offer for sale; or
(*iii*) an offer for sale by tender.

(*b*) *Placing*:

(*i*) A private placing;
(*ii*) a Stock Exchange placing.

(*c*) An *introduction*.
(*d*) A *rights issue*.
(*e*) A *bonus issue*.

All these are methods whereby companies raise new capital (except the introduction and bonus issue) and all, except the private placings, by the issue of quoted securities.

9. An offer for sale. This method either permits a company to raise new capital by means of an issue of shares, or allows existing shareholders to realise their shareholdings in cash. In the former case, the issuing house buys the shares from the company and, in the latter case, from the shareholders. As principal, it offers them for sale to the public, either by offering the shares at the purchase price, charging the company a fee for the Stock Exchange quotation and administrative services, or by reselling them at a higher price, and making a profit on the transaction, or it does both.

10. Preliminary work for an issue. The fifty-six members of the Issuing Houses Association play an important role in the new issues market, acting as intermediaries between companies seeking long-term capital and those who are prepared to supply it by means of investment. Companies desiring quotation seek the sponsorship of a specialist merchant bank whose high standing will inspire the confidence of investors. This is essential for a successful issue. However, before committing its name to the venture, the bank will naturally examine the company very carefully, its memorandum and articles of association, trading record, directors and management, shareholders and its true financial position.

If satisfied, it then works out a programme dealing with the following points:

(*a*) Capital reorganisation schemes.
(*b*) The size of the issue.
(*c*) The timing of the issue.
(*d*) Classes of securities, their terms and the estimated issue prices.

Once these proposals are agreed, then a detailed programme is planned for the preparation of reports by solicitors, accountants and stockbrokers. These are required for the registrar of companies, the Stock Exchange, the prospectus (*see* **11**), publication and advertising.

11. Prospectus. This is the invitation to the public to apply for shares or debentures in the company. Prospectuses are probably familiar to most people, since they are widely advertised in the press. Briefly they contain the following:

(*a*) The name of the company, its share capital, names of directors, bankers, solicitors, auditors, brokers and secretary, and the arrangements for application.
(*b*) The chairman's report, which deals with the following points:

(*i*) History and business.
(*ii*) Management and staff.

(*iii*) Premises.
(*iv*) Net assets employed in the company.
(*v*) Working capital.
(*vi*) Profits and dividends.
(*vii*) Prospects.

(*c*) The accountant's report, which contains the following information:

(*i*) The company's profits (pre-tax and pre-depreciation) for the previous five years.
(*ii*) The company's assets and liabilities.
(*iii*) The rates of dividends paid on each class of share for the past five years.

(*d*) General information, including the following:

(*i*) Directors' interests.
(*ii*) Whether or not the company is a close company.
(*iii*) Articles of association.
(*iv*) Details of subsidiaries.
(*v*) Details of the contract between the shareholders and the issuing house, and other contracts not in the ordinary course of business.
(*vi*) Details of capital reorganisation.

12. The investor decides. Prospective investors who are attracted by the advertisement will decide whether to invest in the company by reference to the following:

(*a*) The company's record of profits. Clearly consistent profit growth is important.

(*b*) The anticipated growth of profits.

(*c*) The degree of safety for dividend payment, *i.e.* dividend cover.

(*d*) The ability of the managers.

(*e*) The industry's growth rate.

(*f*) The ability of the company to exceed this growth rate, bearing in mind the existing and future product range and production facilities.

13. Application and allotment. After the application lists are closed, work proceeds on allotment. If the issue is under-subscribed, then all applications can be accepted in full and the shortfall borne by the underwriters (*see* **14**). In the case of over-subscription, ballots are held or applications scaled down, usually to the advantage of smaller applicants (*see* Table I).

TABLE I.— BASIS OF ALLOTMENT FOR SHARES IN SCOTTISH, ENGLISH AND EUROPEAN TEXTILES (APRIL 1969).

Application	Allotment	Application	Allotment
200– 2,000	200 ballot for shares	50,500–100,000	5,000
2,100– 5,000	200	100,500–200,000	10,000
5,500–10,000	500	200,500–300,000	15,000
10,500–25,000	1,000		
25,000–50,000	2,500	over 300,000	20,000

Source: Financial Times.

Letters of acceptance and allotment are posted so that they are received by the allottees before dealings commence.

14. Underwriting. For a fee, the issuing house underwrites the issue, guaranteeing a full subscription at the agreed terms. Thus the risk to the company, that adverse market conditions might endanger the issue, is removed, since any deficiency in public subscription is made good by the issuing house and its sub-underwriters (other merchant banks, insurance companies, pension funds and other institutional investors) in return for a sub-underwriting commission of about $1\frac{1}{4}$ per cent on the offer price. Thus, of the £20 million Agricultural Mortgage Corporation $9\frac{1}{2}$ per cent debenture stock 1983–6, applications were received for 7 per cent. The remaining 93 per cent were taken up by the underwriters.

In spite of this extreme case, sub-underwriters are apparently in a privileged position. If the issue is fully subscribed, they earn a commission without further obligation on their part, and if not they possess sound quoted securities which are marketable, perhaps eventually at a premium, in addition to their fee.

15. A public issue by the company. Here the company raises capital by offering shares directly to the public. The procedure is much the same as for the offer for sale outlined above. However, in this case the issuing house does not assume the role of principal and is not normally required by the issuing company to deal with advertising, allocation and allotment, although it usually arranges underwriting.

16. Offer for sale by tender. The procedure is similar to that for issuing Government Treasury bills. It has been used by a number of public utilities since 1945 and by other companies throughout the 1960s.

The offer for sale quotes a minimum price to guide investors in tendering a price which they judge will secure for them the allotment they want. However, shares are finally allotted at a single *striking* price, which is the lowest price at which the issue is fully subscribed. Obviously, this is to the advantage of applicants who have quoted excessively high prices.

The extent to which this method has been used has varied according to the issue and the experiences of companies raising capital in this manner. When striking prices are necessarily set below the minimum offer and dealings open at a discount, the attitude of issuing houses and investors to further issues by tender is certain to be influenced. The approval of the Stock Exchange is always required.

17. Advantages of tenders.

(*a*) Tenders may be preferred by issuing houses in unsettled markets or where a company seeking quotation has no counterpart for comparison. By *charging what the market will bear*, they are relieved of the full responsibility for pitching the terms of the issue exactly right and are spared the embarrassment of a large premium should they pitch the offer price too low in an offer for sale.

(*b*) In a buoyant market, an optimistic valuation by the public will mean that vendors may get a better price for their shares. However, they should also consider that they may be driven up to levels which they cannot hold, which could jeopardise future issues.

(*c*) Tenders reduce stagging activities (*see* **18**) because the parties who tender and establish the likely striking price are generally the long-term investors.

In view of these changing conditions, tenders seem to come into vogue for short periods.

18. Stags. The difficulty of issuing successfully a large number of shares or loan stock over a short period is reduced by the activities of stags, who acquire shares for resale at a profit when dealings commence. However, they are most active when the risk of losses from unfavourable changes in market conditions is lowest and may be discouraged if the issuing house believes that permanent investors will subscribe sufficient amounts. Investors who must compete for allotment naturally wish them to be discouraged. They may be discouraged in the following ways:

(*a*) Since stagging is encouraged when part of the issue price is payable on application and the balance by calls, the issuing house can demand payment in full on application.

(*b*) Evidence of sufficient bank facilities to match total applications may be required. Alternatively all cheques may be "presented."

(Thus financial limitations will prevent stags from applying for very large amounts.)

(*c*) Multiple applications, which increase their chances of reasonable allotments in ballots and drastic scaling-down arrangements, may be banned.

(*d*) Banks are unlikely to provide facilities for these purposes in times of severe credit squeeze.

19. Private placings. Companies not requiring quotation, or needing only limited amounts of capital, may approach issuing houses in order to be privately placed. Institutional clients may be more interested in the security of the investment, return and growth, rather than marketability of the securities. Alternatively, companies may place their shares or loan stock direct with interested finance houses.

20. Stock Exchange placings. The Stock Exchange may agree to a placing of securities which are likely to be of limited interest to investors. Small issues of fixed interest securities which fall into this category are placed with institutional investors, brokers and jobbers on the Stock Exchange, from whom the general public may purchase.

21. Costs of new issues. The expenses of placings are substantially less than those for public issues and offers for sale, for the following reasons:

(*a*) Printing costs of limited numbers of application forms and prospectuses are lower.

(*b*) Bank charges for application and allotment are lower.

(*c*) No underwriting is required.

(*d*) Advertising charges are minimal.

The Stock Exchange introduction is certain to be the least costly method.

Costs vary not only between the method of issue, but according to the size of the issue. Naturally a large issue will incur higher charges than a smaller one. However, this is a source of real economies of scale, since costs do not increase in proportion to the size of the issue. Table II shows the economies of large-scale issues.

TABLE II.—ECONOMIES OF LARGE-SCALE ISSUES.

Value of offer for sale	Total cost of issue	%
£210,000	£24,000	11·4
£520,000	£30,000	5·8
£2,000,000	£90,000	4·5

22. Stock Exchange introduction. Where a company's shares are held by, say, 100 shareholders, quotation or *permission to deal* may be obtained by means of an introduction. This does not raise new capital and so does not require a prospectus, although advertisements similar to those for placings are needed. Information is also required by the Shares and Loans Department of the Stock Exchange, as for a quotation of shares by public issue.

23. Rights issue. When raising new capital, companies very commonly give existing shareholders an opportunity to subscribe for shares at a preferential price in proportion to their existing holdings. For instance, in a *one for two* issue, a shareholder with 200 shares is entitled to a further 100.

24. Advantages to the company.

(*a*) A rights issue is relatively cheap and simple.
(*b*) It is usually successful.
(*c*) It provides publicity.
(*d*) Additional shares may create a more active market.

25. Disadvantages to the company.

(*a*) The company may forgo higher premiums obtainable in the open market.
(*b*) It must increase profits proportionally to maintain the dividend rate and share prices.
(*c*) The extra supplies may in the short term depress the share price.

26. Advantages to shareholders.

(*a*) They buy shares at a preferential price if rights are taken up.
(*b*) They can sell rights to third parties. Either way no loss is incurred. (Details of current rights offers are published daily in the *Financial Times*).
(*c*) They may maintain their relative shareholding and control position.
(*d*) They can make up their mind whether to sell or accept on the basis of their past experience with the company.
(*e*) The lower share price may make them more marketable.

27. Disadvantages to shareholders.

(*a*) Those who fail to sell rights or accept will suffer losses from lower share prices. For example:

Already issued: 100,000 ordinary shares
(market value £1) $= £100,000$
Rights issue: 100,000 ordinary shares issued
at 80p $= £80,000$

Total capital: 200,000 ordinary shares $= £180,000$
Therefore 1 ordinary share $= \dfrac{£180,000}{£200,000}$

$= 90p$ per share, compared with the original £1.

Shareholders who accept lose 10p per share on those held, but gain 10p on new shares.

(b) They may lack funds.

(c) They face increased risks arising from their increased shareholding. Diversification may be preferable.

(d) They may incur capital gains liability on the sale of rights.

28. Bonus issues. A bonus issue does not raise fresh capital but represents a capitalisation of accumulated reserves, which brings nominal capital into line with the value of capital employed (e.g. a company, X, with 50,000 £1 shares quoted at £4, and reserves of £150,000, might issue bonus shares in the ratio 3:1). Such issues do not provide the shareholder with any direct monetary advantage, for although he holds more shares, the average price falls (the extent depending on market sentiment) and total dividends are unlikely to change since corporate earning power is unchanged. Nevertheless, the smaller valuation tends to make them slightly more attractive to investors and therefore more marketable. Shareholders' relative voting powers are also unchanged.

29. Timing the issue. There is no set of rules for the timing of issues, a process which is very important for its success. To companies this means the best possible price for their shares and the lowest fixed interest charges on long-term loans. They have to rely to a large extent on the judgment of the issuing house, which can best interpret market trends. There are a multitude of factors which may influence the climate of the market and the success or otherwise of an issue. An issuing house will consider the following factors, in timing an issue:

(a) The general level of prices of securities.

(b) The general market trends and trade expectations.

(c) Political and international crises.

(d) Budgets.

(e) Taxation changes and company legislation.

Table III indicates the relative importance of the main methods employed in the capital market to raise new finance by the issue of quoted securities. Note the insignificance of tenders in comparison with placings, rights issues and offers for sale.

TABLE III.——CAPITAL ISSUES BY QUOTED PUBLIC COMPANIES
ANALYSED BY METHOD OF ISSUE (£m).

	1967	1968	1969	1970	1971	1972	1973
Public issues and offers for sale	74·5	30·6	112·3	28·6	102·3	293·7	93·3
Tenders	2·1	10·2	9·9	37·2	34·3	24·4	8·0
Placings	303·1	178·4	139·3	140·2	253·4	323·3	89·6
Issues to shareholders:							
(a) Ordinary shares	64·2	362·4	169·4	62·7	169·9	359·1	71·0
(b) Preference and loan capital	74·6	107·6	197·0	92·6	66·1	116·7	26·5

Source: Bank of England Bulletin.

OTHER LONG-TERM SOURCES

30. Sale and lease-back. Since the late 1950s, sale and lease-back of property has been increasingly used by firms as a method of raising capital. Sales of property to institutions interested in long-term investments (insurance companies and pension funds) may benefit the company in the following ways:

(a) It releases tied-up capital badly needed for other purposes. Ideally, this should produce a return in excess of the leasing and its alternative, the net return on funds borrowed against the property.

(b) Long-term tenure is guaranteed.

(c) The rental may be offset against taxation.

On the debit side, however, it may be less attractive to the firm in the long run, since the sale may produce the following drawbacks:

(a) The loss of a valuable asset, which is certain to appreciate with inflation and is acceptable security for loans.

(b) A liability for capital gains tax.

(c) Periodic rent reviews (every seven years) will increase the rentals if inflation persists.

(d) The trader is still responsible for the costs of insurance and repair.

31. Financing industry by hire purchase (H.P.). This is an increasingly important source of medium-term finance for the purchase of capital goods, ranging from plant and equipment to commodities and vehicles and their insurance. Instalment credit extended by finance houses for industrial plant and equipment stood at £21 million in 1958, £113 million in 1967 and £2,732 million in 1977 (Department of Trade estimates).

32. Types of H.P. agreement.

(a) *Ordinary H.P. agreement.* The seller invoices the goods to the H.P. company, which agrees with the customer on a charge to be added to the amount financed. This *balance of hire* is then repaid in equal instalments by the customer over, say, twenty-four months.

(b) *Machine life finance.* This recent innovation in the U.K. allows customers to purchase equipment over its anticipated working life. Once this is agreed, periodic payments are calculated by adding to the reducing balance a percentage finance charge which is linked to, and slightly above, minimum lending rate.

33. The H.P. rate of interest.

Any person or organisation contemplating buying equipment or goods on H.P. should be aware that the real rate of interest charged by the H.P. company is certain to be a good deal higher than the stated percentage. This is because the latter is based on the original sum borrowed when in fact each instalment reduces the borrowed sum; over the life of the H.P. agreement the average sum borrowed is only about half of the original amount outstanding. For instance, if the contract is for the repayment of the original sum by twenty-four equal payments at an annual rate of interest of 10 per cent, the true rate of interest is:

$$\frac{\text{Annual stated rate} \times 2 \times \text{No. of instalments}}{\text{No. of instalments} + 1}$$

$$= \frac{10 \times 2 \times 24}{25}$$

$$= 19 \cdot 2\%$$

34. Advantages of H.P. agreements.

Advocates of H.P. financing point out the following advantages:

(a) H.P. encourages firms to take a longer-term view of investment requirements, since they no longer have to buy only when they have sufficient funds for outright purchase.

(*b*) It is the use of equipment which is important for profits and this is gained on payment of the first instalment.

(*c*) Since capital is not tied up immediately, it may find alternative profitable employment.

(*d*) The instalment charges are predetermined.

(*e*) Fixed instalments are advantageous in inflation.

(*f*) A variety of flexible H.P. agreements are available to suit the customer.

(*g*) Interest payments are tax deductable.

Legally, finance houses are entitled to re-possess goods if the terms of the agreement are broken. Consequently, they are generally reluctant to finance the purchase of equipment in this way, if it becomes a fixture within a building, or it has restricted marketability; *e.g.* furnaces (where a secured loan is more suitable). Instead they favour identifiable goods with working lives exceeding the term of the agreement.

35. Leasing. The post-war practice of renting equipment from finance houses is now well established in the U.K. It has long been a method of equipping business offices, but latterly, with the development of complex and costly equipment which needs regular servicing, firms have taken advantage of leasing schemes. The parties negotiate a primary lease period of between three and seven years, according to the anticipated working life of the equipment, in which time the capital cost and service charges are recouped. Thereafter, for the indefinite secondary period, the lessee may continue to use the equipment at a nominal rental.

36. Differences between H.P. and leasing. Lease and H.P. financing have many advantages in common, although there are the following basic differences:

(*a*) The whole leasing rental is tax allowable compared to just the interest charge of H.P.

(*b*) Unlike H.P. financing, it is the finance house which receives any investment grant payable for qualifying equipment, although it can pass on these benefits to the lessee by way of lower rental charges.

(*c*) The title never passes to the lessee; *i.e.* there is no option to purchase.

(*d*) Deposits are not required.

(*e*) Leasing agreements are not borrowings, and so do not limit a company's borrowing powers.

(*f*) The lessee may use the equipment after the first payment.

SHORT-TERM, AND SPECIALISED FINANCE FOR INDUSTRY

SHORT-TERM FINANCE

37. Trade credit. It is an impossible task to measure accurately the value of credit that firms advance their customers. Nevertheless, the *Radcliffe Report* 1959, indicated that the total amount of trade credit outstanding surpassed the total of bank credit. If this is true today (and there is no reason to think otherwise) trade credit exceeds £30,351 million (1974). Little is known about its distribution pattern, but it is thought that it is relatively more important to small firms and fast-growing firms. The latter are likely to be net-takers, as their need for working capital runs ahead of their resources. Larger firms on the other hand are perhaps able to economise on working capital, holding a smaller proportion to turnover.

38. Forms of trade credit. Credit terms, which vary between businesses, may be arranged as follows:

(*a*) They may be recommended by the industrial trade association.

(*b*) They may be a trade custom.

(*c*) They may be specially arranged by the parties. For example:

   (*i*) customers may advance loans to manufacturers to buy materials;

   (*ii*) customers may supply manufacturers with materials (to guarantee quality), paying for manufacturing costs with an allowance for materials wastage (*i.e. free issue materials*);

   (*iii*) customers may advance loans towards the costs of equipment.

39. Cost of trade credit. There are costs to firms giving and taking credit as follows:

(*a*) Although invoices are usually submitted *terms net monthly*, it may in practice be six weeks before settlement is made. This costs the creditor more than 1·5 per cent (if annual interest is taken as 12 per cent) in addition to the accounting and collection costs. There is evidence that firms are beginning to consider the opportunity cost of this credit, *i.e.* profitable alternative uses to which this money can be put, as judged from the growth of factoring services.

(*b*) Customers who take credit and thereby waive cash discounts forgo returns which for large-scale purchases may amount to substantial sums per annum. Thus a purchaser who is offered a cash discount of 2·5 per cent if payment is made within seven days, or alternatively full payment within thirty days, is really paying 40·9 per cent interest for the credit by deciding not to pay cash; for example:

Cost of credit

$$= \frac{\text{percentage discount}}{100 - \text{percentage discount}}$$
$$\times \frac{365}{\text{final payment date} - \text{period of discount}} \times 100$$
$$= \frac{2 \cdot 5}{97 \cdot 5} \times \frac{365}{23}$$
$$= 40 \cdot 6\%$$

Clearly the firm should borrow to take advantage of the cash discount.

40. Risks. Dependence on trade credit carries the following risks:

(*a*) Middlemen may find themselves in an impossible dilemma when placed between creditors, who withdraw or grant credit on less liberal terms, and their customers, who may also attempt to reduce their credit terms.

(*b*) As a result, customer goodwill is lost.

(*c*) Reliance on powerful creditors might result in a loss of independence.

41. Bank credit. British commercial banks do not generally advance long-term loans, which would conflict with their basic objectives of security and liquidity of funds. However, although theoretically repayable on demand, overdrafts are generally renewable by negotiation and constitute a flexible and an important source of working capital for the financing of materials, work in progress, finished stocks and debtors.

Furthermore, interest rates are relatively low and, coupled with the fact that the borrower only pays for money used, represent a cheap form of finance.

42. Rates of interest. The rates charged to a businessman will be influenced by the following factors:

(a) The current base rate, to which overdraft and loan rates are linked (bank base rate plus $1\frac{1}{2}$ to 3 per cent).

(b) The credit-worthiness of the borrower, which will depend on:

(i) the records of profits;
(ii) the relation of assets to liabilities;
(iii) borrowers' integrity and commercial goodwill; and
(iv) the quality of available collateral and securities.

43. Classification of bankers' advances. The importance of bank credit to the various sectors of the British economy is indicated in Table IV.

TABLE IV.—CLASSIFICATION OF BANKERS' ADVANCES.

Type of customer	£m Nov. 72	(%)	£m Feb. 74	(%)
Manufacturing sector	4,771	20·25	7,328	18·17
Extractive, agriculture and construction	1,861	7·90	3,221	7·98
Personal sector	2,635	11·18	4,009	9·94
Service sector	3,111	13·21	5,866	14·54
Financial institutions	3,370	14·31	7,031	17·43
Overseas	7,802	33·12	2,724	31·55
Total advances	23,550		40,179	

Source: Barclays Bank Review (May 1974).

44. Bank bill finance. Bank bills of exchange are drawn on acceptance of credit facilities granted by merchant banks to their customers, preferably against short-term self-liquidating transactions, which realise funds to meet the bills at maturity. They are termed *fine* bills as their payment is guaranteed and they are second only to Treasury bills for the lowest rate of discount when sold by the customer in the discount market. Thus they offer the businessman a relatively cheap and reliable source of short-term credit.

45. Trade bills. This is a bill of exchange drawn by a trader on another in exchange for goods where the purchaser is granted a period of credit and makes payment on its maturity. However, should the creditor want immediate payment, then he sells (discounts) the bill, and the purchaser of the bill receives the full sum on the due date. His success and the cost charged by the purchaser of the bill for advancing payment will depend on the following factors:

(*a*) *The general financial and commercial standing* of both parties to the transaction.

(*b*) *The nature of the transaction.* There are no obstacles if the parties customarily finance their business by bills. However, banks may refuse to discount accommodation bills which are issued without valid consideration.

(*c*) *The number of bills* already in the discount market and particularly those bearing the acceptor's name. As a result of these factors, the differential on trade bills can be as low as 0·5 per cent and as high as 2 per cent a year.

Generally speaking, bills of exchange are becoming less important as a source of credit, although they are still widely used in certain areas, *e.g.* commodity markets.

46. The choice of finance. An increasing number of companies are turning their attention to the London money market for the investment of surplus cash and to extend their lines of credit to augment their traditional overdraft facilities. A study of the *Money Market* section in the *Financial Times* illustrates the range of financial services provided by the banks in the market. An extract from this section is as follows:

April 11th 1974	*£ certs. of deposit*	*Finance house deposits*	*Company deposits*	*Discount house deposits*	*Bank bills*	*Fine trade bills*
Overnight	—	—	$12\frac{3}{4}$	$9-12\frac{1}{2}$	—	—
7 days	—	$13\frac{1}{4}$	—	$11\frac{1}{2}-11\frac{3}{4}$	—	—
1 month	$13\frac{1}{8}-12\frac{7}{8}$	$13\frac{3}{8}-13\frac{3}{4}$	—	$11\frac{3}{4}-12$	$13\frac{1}{8}-13\frac{3}{8}$	$13\frac{1}{8}-14\frac{1}{2}$
2 months	$13\frac{1}{2}-13\frac{3}{8}$	$13\frac{5}{8}-14$	—	$11\frac{3}{4}-12$	$13\frac{5}{16}-13\frac{5}{8}$	$13\frac{1}{2}-14\frac{1}{2}$
3 months	$13\frac{11}{16}-13\frac{1}{2}$	$13\frac{5}{8}-14$	—	12	$13\frac{5}{16}-13\frac{1}{2}$	$13\frac{1}{2}-14\frac{1}{2}$
6 months	$13\frac{3}{4}-13\frac{5}{8}$	$13\frac{5}{8}-14$	—	—	$13\frac{1}{4}-13\frac{3}{4}$	$13\frac{1}{4}-14\frac{1}{2}$
9 months	$13\frac{3}{4}-13\frac{1}{2}$	—	—	—	—	—
1 year	$13\frac{13}{16}-13\frac{5}{8}$	—	—	—	—	—
2 years	$13\frac{7}{8}-13\frac{1}{2}$	—	—	—	—	—

FIG. 1.—Sources of finance and terms of credit.

NOTES:

(*i*) Bank of England minimum lending rate is 12 per cent.

(*ii*) Finance house base rate is $15\frac{1}{2}$ per cent since April 1st.

(*iii*) Clearing bank deposit rate is $9\frac{1}{4}$ per cent for small sums requiring seven days notice of withdrawal.

(*iv*) Clearing bank base rate for lending is $12\frac{1}{2}$ per cent.

(*v*) Sterling certificates of deposit are certificates issued by banks against deposits. They are negotiable, *i.e.* can be readily sold in the market and thereby allow depositors to obtain high yields without corresponding reductions in liquidity.

(*vi*) Finance house deposits and discount house deposits provide investment opportunities for individuals and companies. The former is used to finance their investment, hire purchase and leasing work and the latter to finance the purchasing of bills of exchange.

(*vii*) Company deposits are made available by companies that temporarily have funds to spare to other companies that temporarily need funds.

(*viii*) Bank bills and fine trade bills are bills of exchange (*see* **44** and **45**).

The above extract shows that:

(*a*) Generally rates of interest move with the length of time money is locked up. Thus on money deposited overnight in the discount houses the minimum rate is some 9 per cent, but 12 per cent is offered on money deposited for three months to compensate for the increased risk. However, sterling certificate of deposit rates are lower over two years indicating that the market anticipates market interest rates to fall in the future.

(*b*) Companies with surplus funds or wishing to borrow can select the term of the deposit or loan that meets their individual requirements.

(*c*) Companies can compare the relative rates of interest for borrowing or depositing and select that which minimises the cost or maximises the return. Indeed, there is ample evidence that companies know their way around this market judging from the development of arbitrage, *i.e.* borrowing at cheap overdraft rates for more profitable reinvestment in this market.

47. Invoice discounting. Expanding companies often find that rising sales bring increased book debts. However, there are today a number of firms prepared to advance finance to alleviate the problem of insufficient liquidity which hinders further growth, by invoice discounting. Generally an invoice discounting facility is agreed for sound established traders who "offer" to sell to the specialist sales debts up to this limit and who guarantee the payment of any debts so bought. If the offer is accepted, then the trader receives a cheque for perhaps 75 per cent of the total amount and accepts a bill of exchange for the same amount as security for his guarantee. He then acts as the specialist's agent, collecting sales debts in the usual manner to honour the bill. The following advantages are claimed for the trader:

(a) *The increased liquidity* will mean that the trader can take advantage of cash discounts offered by suppliers which may exceed the overall cost of the facility, which is about 1 per cent per month.

(b) *Greater credit terms* can be extended to customers.

(c) *More working capital* is available for peak production periods in seasonal trades.

(d) *Improved credit rating* through prompter payments.

(e) Since the trader may use the facility at his option, it may be a *more economical source of finance* than fixed interest loans.

48. Factoring. Factoring, established in Britain in 1959, is similar to invoice discounting in that the specialist advances finance when it buys a trader's book debts, but in addition it may assume responsibility for the sales ledger and the credit risk. Naturally, the cost varies accordingly. The cost of the cash flow may be base rate plus 2 per cent, in addition to the service charge which will vary between 0·5 and 2 per cent on turnover, depending on:

(a) the size of the company;

(b) the amount of work (*i.e.* the number of invoices); and

(c) the degree of risk.

In 1974 the value of factoring amounted to £300 million.

49. Advantages of factoring. The main advantages to a firm using the services of a factor may be summarised as follows:

(*a*) There are *clerical and administrative savings*, particularly for firms selling repetitively on credit, as follows:

(*i*) In effect the firm has one customer only, the factor. Even if the factor is "undisclosed" to the firm's customers, it is a simple matter for the firm to endorse cheques and pass them on.

(*ii*) The firm is no longer concerned with bad debt controls.

(*iii*) There are economies in management and staff salaries, since fewer supervisors and clerical workers are needed. Also there are corresponding savings in recruitment and training.

(*b*) There are also the following *financial benefits*:

(*i*) Capital locked up in sundry debtors' balances is available for use within the business, as all sales in effect become cash sales.

(*ii*) With this improved liquidity it can offer improved credit terms to its customers in order to increase orders.

(*iii*) It can take advantage of suppliers' cash discount and make prompt payments.

(*iv*) This improves its credit rating.

(*v*) The turnover of stocks into cash is speeded up and this allows a larger turnover on the same investment.

(*vi*) Undisclosed factoring does not prejudice customer goodwill.

(*vii*) Since factoring is not borrowing, the company's balance sheet liquidity is not weakened nor its borrowing potential impaired.

These administrative and financial savings may be more than sufficient to cover the cost of the factoring service.

(*c*) The company is free to concentrate on the main jobs of *producing and selling*.

50. Financing of retail sales by H.P. Many retailers selling goods on a hire purchase or rental basis use the services of the many specialists in this field, so as to maintain the liquidity of working capital. The retailer has a choice of either placing the customer with the H.P. company to draw up the agreement and arrange the payments of instalments direct, or of using "block" discounting facilities where he sells his H.P. debts for an immediate payment of a high proportion of the value of H.P. sales. The retailer than collects the instalment in the normal way to repay the finance company. Today, H.P.

financing has reached an enormous scale: £556 million in 1958, £1,269 million in 1968 and £2,451 million in 1973.

SPECIALISED FINANCE

51. The Industrial and Commercial Finance Corporation. The Industrial and Commercial Finance Corporation was formed by the Bank of England and the Scottish and English commercial banks in 1945. In 1974 the I.C.F.C. merged with the Finance Corporation for Industry to form Finance for Industry Ltd. The purpose of the I.C.F.C. is to assist small- and medium-sized companies and "to provide credit and finance by means of loans or the subscription of loan or share capital or otherwise, for industrial and commercial businesses or enterprises in Great Britain." Finance from £5,000 to £500,000, to suit the requirements of the borrower, at competitive rates of interest, is available in the following variety of forms:

(a) *Secured loans and debentures.*
(b) *Unsecured loans.*
(c) *Redeemable preference shares.*
(d) *Irredeemable preference shares.*
(e) *Ordinary shares.*
(f) *A plant purchase scheme*, which enables customers to purchase plant and equipment by means of a hire purchase transaction over periods of up to five years.
(g) *Leasing facilities*, available for customers who wish to use new capital equipment without tying up finance in capital investment.

In addition, the I.C.F.C. operates a management advisory service, arranges issues and floatations and gives assistance on mergers through its subsidiary, Industrial Mergers Ltd. and operates an expert advisory service.

52. Summary of I.C.F.C. assistance. Since its inception, the business of the I.C.F.C. has grown substantially. It has provided financial assistance of some £330 million to more than 2,300 companies engaged in a wide range of activities throughout Great Britain. Table V shows the finance provided by way of secured and unsecured loans, ordinary and preference shares and leasing and plant purchase facilities.

Furthermore, the continuing interest shown by the I.C.F.C. in the small- and medium-sized firm is indicated by the "positively skewed" frequency table, where amounts outstanding of £5,000 to £50,000 figure prominently. Note that "positively skewed" means that advances are initially high and then tail off.

TABLE V.—EXAMPLE OF I.C.F.C. ASSISTANCE.

Classification of financial facilities by amounts outstanding at 31st March 1968 and 1977,		
	Customers	
	1968	1977
Up to £10,000	386	449
£10,001– 20,000	302	325
£20,001– 50,000	419	582
	1,107	1,356
£50,001–100,000	289	356
£100,001–200,000	250	261
£200,001–300,000 ⎫		91
£300,001–500,000 ⎬	42	76
£500,001 and over ⎭		61
Total	1,688	2,201

Source: I.C.F.C. Annual Report.

53. The Agricultural Mortgage Corporation Ltd. This was established in 1928 with the Bank of England and other banks as its shareholders. Its objectives are to assist the farming industry by granting the following loans:

(a) Long-term loans on agricultural land and buildings.

(b) Loans for improvements to farms from funds. These are derived from:

(i) Loans and grants from the Ministry of Agriculture and Fisheries; or (*ii*) issues of debentures on the open market at competitive rates. The exceptionally high market rates of 1968–9 demanded very high coupons. Even so, 93 per cent of an issue at 9½ per cent was left with underwriters and contributed to a further increase in their loan rates to another all-time high of 10·5 per cent. To date, its loan totals exceed £100 million.

54. The Ship Mortgage Finance Co. Ltd. This was founded in 1951 with its share capital subscribed by the shipbuilding industry, insurance companies and various finance companies. Its aim is to finance the construction of ships in British yards. It is managed by the I.C.F.C. Since its inception, it has contributed some £24 million from its own funds and found participants for a further £17 million. Its work is not entirely to finance. It uses its specialised knowledge to manage shipping lines owned by the I.C.F.C. and it acts on behalf of the Minister of Technology in assessing the credit-worthiness of shipyards which request grants under the *Shipbuilding Industry Act* 1967.

55. The Finance Corporation for Industry Ltd. The F.C.I. was set up with government encouragement in 1945 with 40 per cent of its capital held by insurance companies and 30 per cent each by the bank and investment trusts. Its object is the lending of £200,000 or more by secured or unsecured loans to businesses requiring urgent funds for re-equipment or development. Priority has been given where funds are otherwise unobtainable on reasonable terms and to projects deemed to be in the national interest, particularly in the mining, steel, chemical, electrical and textile industries. Since 1945 the F.C.I. has advanced some £30 million to British industry and at March 1977 its outstanding loans stood at £241 million.

56. The Technical Development Capital Ltd. The T.D.C., a commercial enterprise acquired by the I.C.F.C. in 1966, was set up in 1962 with shareholders from merchant banks and British and Commonwealth insurance companies. This followed the recommendation of the Radcliffe Report on the workings of the British monetary system for an institution to supply finance for the development of technical innovations. The T.D.C. is not intended to finance basic research like the National Research Development Corporation, but supplies risk capital for the later stages of development, production and marketing. It has no fixed method of financing, but negotiates terms on an individual basis. However, it expects a shareholding, in addition to any loan it makes, to compensate for the substantial financial risks, and since its object is to aid innovators, its policy is not to hold them permanently, but to sell once the venture is established. Currently, it has investments of £90 million in some 1,500 companies widely distributed throughout industry.

57. The Estate Duties Investment Trust Ltd. "Edith" was formed in 1952 by insurance companies and investment trusts and is managed by the I.C.F.C.; it went public in 1962. It is ready to acquire minority holdings in soundly-run private or small public companies without seeking to control management. The main benefits to the company's shareholders are as follows:

(*a*) Even though the market for their shares is restricted, they have access to funds.

(*b*) Company control is unaffected.

(*c*) Aged shareholders have liquid funds for payment of death duty, although capital gains tax liability may arise.

(*d*) Death duty liability is reduced if these funds are used:

(*i*) to purchase annuities;

(*ii*) for inter-vivos gifts (seven years before death to be tax free); or

(*iii*) to acquire assets which carry a lower rate of duty, *e.g.* forestry land.

At March 1977 it had invested a total of £1·5 million.

58. The National Research Development Corporation. The N.R.D.C. was set up in 1945 for "securing, where the public interest so requires, the development and exploitation of inventions resulting from public research and of any other invention which it appears to the corporation is not being exploited or sufficiently developed or exploited." In 1977 submissions totalled 1,780 and 194 were accepted.

The N.R.D.C., which may borrow up to £50 million for this

purpose, should balance its revenue account in the long term. It will grant financial help if it is satisfied that:

(a) the project is technologically feasible;
(b) it stands a good chance of commercial success; and
(c) the company possesses adequate resources and management to exploit the invention.

A typical arrangement is where the N.R.D.C. agrees to buy part of the invoiced development costs and is repaid later by a levy on the sales of the product. The company may offset this against trading profits. Such assistance averages between £7 million and £8 million annually and licence income totalled £15·2 million in 1977 (of which much was earned in foreign currency). An invention which earned significant revenue for the N.R.D.C. was the new anti-biotic Cephalosporin.

59. Other institutions.

(a) *The Charterhouse Group.* This important financial group will supply capital, preferably on a large scale (£50,000 to £250,000), in return for equity and preference and loan stock. In addition, it offers a comprehensive range of specialist financial services for industry.

(b) *The United Dominions Trust.*

(c) *Hambros* (merchant bank).

(d) *Bowmakers.*

60. How these funds are used.

In this chapter we have examined the long- and short-term, and specialised sources of finance, and we now summarise their inter-relationships by showing how these sources are employed by companies (*see* Table VI).

Table VI is constructed on the basis of the most typical source of finance for each Balance Sheet item (and obviously does not provide an exclusive list) and on the tenet of investment that the loan and the use to which it is put must match. Thus, short-term sources ought not be used to finance fixed assets which are by nature long-term investments.

TABLE VI.—RELATIONSHIP BETWEEN THE BALANCE SHEET
AND SOURCES OF FINANCE.

Employment of capital	Source of funds
Fixed assets	
Land and buildings	Mortgage, sale and leaseback
Plant and equipment ⎫	
Furniture and fittings ⎬	H.P., leasing
Motor vehicles ⎭	
Current assets	
Stocks	Overdraft, bill of exchange
Debtors	Overdraft, invoice discounting, factoring

Capital employed	
Share capital	
Ordinary shares ⎫	Company promotors, stock exchange,
Preference shares ⎭	specialised finance companies
Loan capital	
Loan stock ⎫	Stock exchange, insurance companies,
Debentures ⎭	pension funds, banks, specialised finance companies
Current liabilities	
Creditors	Trade credit
Bank overdraft	Commercial banks

PROGRESS TEST 2

1. Explain why so many companies seek quotation for their shares. (3–7)

2. Outline the pros and cons of the methods of issues available to companies. (8–29)

3. Compare and contrast sale and lease-back, H.P. and leasing as sources of finance. (30–36)

4. What is trade credit? (37–39)

5. Compare and contrast invoice discounting and factoring as sources of short term funds. (47–49)

6. Outline the nature and scope of services offered by companies providing "specialised finance." (51–60)

CHAPTER III

MONEY: HOW DO WE RECORD IT?

THE BACKGROUND OF ACCOUNTING

1. Early accounting systems. Archaeologists have discovered that Egyptian, Greek and Roman traders possessed accounting systems that enabled them to assess their trading performance, to control employees and agents and to provide information for management decision making. Thus accounting is not a recent innovation but has existed, albeit in simple form, for several thousands of years. Since then this elementary accounting system of record and control has developed piecemeal to meet the specific needs of the time.

2. The "Italian Method." The modern *double entry* accounting system dates back to the "Italian Method" employed by Italian merchants as early as the fifteenth century and described in detail by Luca Pacioli in 1494. Their system was the product of recording systems encountered by earlier Italian merchants throughout the trading world, and suitably developed to record the dual nature of transactions. This means that for every creditor there is a debtor, for sellers there are corresponding buyers; thus every transaction has a two-fold nature so that for every debit there is a corresponding credit. The outcome is a comprehensive accounting system that records a complete history of transactions for each type of expense, asset and liability in the appropriate account which can be built up into statements showing trading performance and financial position. Furthermore, its dual aspect provides a self-balancing facility and a check on the book-keeper's accuracy in posting entries.

3. The accountant. Two groups of specialist accountants emerged in the U.K. They are:

(*a*) *The accountant in public practice.* The *Companies Acts* from the mid-nineteenth century regulating the affairs of joint stock companies demanded that an auditor should report on the company's Balance Sheet presented by the directors to the shareholders. Professional accountants carried out these duties, and in time extended their interests into company formation, reconstruction, take-overs, winding up and taxation.

(*b*) The accountant in industry acts as a supplier and interpreter of financial information and advises on the financial aspects of management problems. There are two aspects of industrial accountancy:

(*i*) *Financial accountancy*. Here the accountant is concerned with historical financial data, and the application of accounting principles in the preparation of company accounts. In particular, he is concerned with the preparation of the Balance Sheet, the directors' report and Profit and Loss Account which are presented to people outside the company. In addition to shareholders, the Inland Revenue and the Registrar of Companies have copies of a company's accounts.

(*ii*) *Management accountancy*. Here the accountant is responsible for the generation of costing and financial data, interpretation of information and the preparation of forecasts. His purpose is to examine company financial affairs from the viewpoint of management and serve as an information manager to help management make more effective decisions.

4. The joint stock company. A company is a legal person which can employ people to work for it, own property, be a creditor or debtor, sue on its own behalf and of course be sued. Its identity is distinct from that of the shareholders who pool their financial resources to set up the company and who thereby jointly own the company's stock, holding shares in the company in proportion to their contributions to the company's capital.

The joint stock company dates back to the seventeenth century. Among the earliest were the East India Company and Hudson's Bay Company created by Royal Charter. In 1844 the *Joint Stock Companies Act* allowed promoters to form companies by registration with the Registrar of Companies, and in 1855 parliament granted limited liability for shareholders.

5. Advantages of a company. The joint stock company

possesses significant advantages over other forms of business,
i.e. sole traders and partnerships:

(*a*) It can raise more finance by issuing additional shares.
Sole traders and partnerships are restricted to the financial
backing of the owners.

(*b*) Its legal entity and the transferability of members'
shares mean that it remains in existence after the death of
shareholders. The death of sole traders and partners means
the dissolution of the business.

(*c*) The success of the company does not depend on the
managerial ability of its members for it can employ specialists. Sole traders and partners are managers in their businesses regardless of their managerial talents.

(*d*) It does not suffer the disadvantage of partnerships
where each partner is an agent of other partners and therefore liable for the debts or wrongs committed by other
partners in the ordinary course of business, except in the
case of limited partnerships.

(*e*) The limited liability joint stock company possesses one
very important advantage. The liability of its members is
limited to the amount, if any, unpaid on their shares.
Clearly this is conducive to the raising of capital. However,
it is worth noting that partners may have limited liability
under the 1907 *Limited Partnership Act* but only if they take
no part in the firm's management.

6. Capital of the company. The following terms are used in
connection with the capital of the company:

(*a*) *Shares.* A share is "the interest of a shareholder in a
company measured by a sum of money for the purpose of
liability in the first place and of interest in the second."

(*i*) It represents the investment by the shareholder in the
company. However, in the event of liquidation the investor
stands to lose this amount.

(*ii*) It represents the shareholders' interest in the company
and carries rights to share in distributions of profits and
perhaps to vote at members' meetings.

(*iii*) Shares may be *preference*, *i.e.* receiving a fixed dividend
prior to dividend payments to ordinary shareholders. However, they tend to have little or no voting rights.

(*iv*) Shares may be *ordinary*, with deferred rights to

dividend and voting powers to compensate for the greater risks associated with this investment.

(*b*) *Nominal capital*. This is the total amount of capital that the company is authorised to raise under its Memorandum of Association (basically the rules of the company drawn up by its founders). It is the estimated amount the company will need to meet its objectives.

(*c*) *Issued capital*. This is that part of the authorised capital which has been issued by shares.

(*d*) *Paid up capital*. This is the amount that has been realised by the issue of shares. Today most shares are issued fully paid, but to illustrate the relationships between nominal, issued and paid up capital, we assume the capital of XY Limited to be:

Capital of XY Ltd. at 31.12.71		*31.12.72*
Nominal capital		
1,000,000 Ordinary shares at £1	£1,000,000	£1,000,000
Issued capital		
500,000 Ordinary shares at £1	£500,000	£500,000
Paid-up capital		
500,000 Ordinary shares, 50p paid on each share	£250,000	£500,000 (fully paid)

Thus the company has issued half of its authorised share capital (£500,000 out of a maximum £1,000,000 worth of shares). On 31.12.71 shareholders had subscribed £250,000 or 50p per share and by 31.12.72 had paid the balance of 50p per share so that the issued and paid up capital coincide at £500,000. Should the company require additional capital at a later stage, however, then all or part of the remaining unissued authorised capital could be issued.

(*e*) *Loan capital*. This consists of loans, debentures and mortgages, advanced by individuals and financial organisations. It must be emphasised that these parties are not shareholders but company creditors and consequently receive interest and not dividends on their loans.

(*i*) A debenture security is a written acknowledgement of a debt incurred by a joint stock company. It provides for repayment of the debt with a fixed interest, usually twice yearly. A debenture may be either secured on company assets or unsecured.

(*ii*) A mortgage is similar to a debenture in that it is a loan secured by assets of the borrower, but it differs in that it is a debt to a single lender, the mortgagee. The provision of mortgages is especially well known in the private sector, but it is also a valuable source of long-term capital for commercial undertakings. Insurance companies, pension funds and finance companies are the main mortgagees, although limited funds are available from solicitors and building societies. Organisations like the Ship Mortgage Finance Company and the Agricultural Mortgage Corporation make special-purpose loans.

DUTIES AND RESPONSIBILITIES OF ACCOUNTANTS

7. The management accountant and accounting principles. The management accountant examines the financial aspects of the organisation from the viewpoint of management. Thus management accounting records and reports are for internal use only (and probably for the confidential use of management).

(*a*) They are for information or guidance of management.

(*b*) They are specific to the problem or area under consideration.

(*c*) They cover a period of operations determined by management.

Thus management accounting records and reports do not conform to a generally accepted system of accounting rules. Their purpose, to improve management performance, demands that they are not constrained by rules but are flexible in coverage, timing and are pertinent to the matter under consideration.

8. The financial accountant, auditor and accounting principles. On the other hand, financial accounts are published for a variety of readers (trades unions, creditors, competitors, present and prospective shareholders, the Inland Revenue, investment analysts, etc.). The diversity of their interests means that the reports must be comprehensive, covering all aspects of the organisation and must refer to a predetermined period, normally one trading year. The purpose of financial reports is to provide accurate information on the company's

III. MONEY: HOW DO WE RECORD IT?   43

trading results and financial position. The following accounting rules attempt to satisfy this requirement:

(a) *The accounts must be objective.* In other words, the
accounts must be "true" if based on verifiable evidence.
Whenever estimated data is employed the accountant must
necessarily express a subjective judgment. Above all, such
judgments must be "fair" if they are unbiased. Thus in
summary, the reports must be "true and fair."

(b) *They must be consistent.* This means that ideally the
accounts should be presented and valuations made in the
way customary for that trade. Furthermore they should be
consistent over a period of time. Consequently, valid
comparisons may be made with previous years' accounts and
between companies.

(c) *They should be conservative.* Prudency should be
observed in assessing profits on the grounds that it would
be reckless to include profits before they are realised.
Similarly all liabilities current and contingent should be
anticipated.

(d) *Companies Act requirements.* Legislation requires disclosure by companies in their published accounts of information needed by shareholders to assess the financial state of
their company and the deployment of their funds. These
Company Law requirements are described in detail in
Chapter VIII.

9. Appointment of auditors. The public accountant as
auditor is appointed and his remuneration determined by the
company at each annual general meeting to hold office for the
following year. He must be a member of a recognised body of
accountants, if the company is a public one, and may not be
a director or officer of the company.

10. Responsibilities of the public accountant. The auditor is
a representative of the shareholders and has a duty to report
on the accounts presented by the directors to the company in
general meeting. His report must state:

(a) Whether proper books of account have been kept by
the company.

(b) Whether the Balance Sheet and Profit and Loss

Account represents a true and fair view of the company's financial position and if not in what respects it fails to do so.

11. Rights of public accountants. The auditor has the following rights:

(*a*) Access at all times to the company's books.

(*b*) Information and explanations from company officials for the purpose of the audit.

(*c*) To attend all general meetings and to receive notice of these meetings.

(*d*) To speak at the meetings on the subject of the audit.

(*e*) He has no right to force directors to amend their accounts. However, he may qualify his own report accordingly.

12. Liability of public accounts. The auditor has the following liabilities:

(*a*) *Common law liability.* The auditor must use reasonable skill and diligence in the performance of his duties and may be held liable for any losses arising from his negligence.

(*b*) *Criminal liability.* The auditor may be fined or imprisoned if found guilty of the following:

(*i*) Wilfully making false statements in any report, certificate or balance sheet (*Companies Act* 1948).

(*ii*) Reckless statements made in a prospectus which turn out to be false (*Prevention of Fraud (Investments) Act* 1958).

(*iii*) Stealing, obtaining money by deception, destroying or defacing accounting records, publishing false information (*Theft Act* 1968).

13. Responsibilities of the industrial accountant. The financial accountant is directly responsible for the preparation of the *stewardship* accounts required by company law, *i.e.* for safeguarding the shareholders' money and showing that they are correctly recorded and accounted for.

The management accountant is an employee of the company, a financial information manager, who, together with other managers of administration, production and sales, etc., is responsible for the overall efficient operation of the company and the achievement of its declared objectives. His main contributions lie in the establishing of systems for the measurement of costs, prices, profits and cash flow.

The following are typical examples of the management accountant's work:

(a) Measurement of costs of products, departments, methods and equipment.

(b) The matching of cash resources with company requirements, *i.e.* cash planning and control.

(c) Preparation of budgets.

(d) Measurement of profitabilities of products, departments and the general economic performance of the organisation.

14. Liabilities of the industrial accountant. The management accountant's liabilities are less onerous than those of the financial accountant who has direct and specific responsibilities to the shareholders. Indeed his liabilities are those of the auditor outlined above. The management accountant however is not bound by the principles of stewardship accounting, and therefore avoids the stringent requirements of the *Companies Act* and the *Prevention of Fraud* (*Investment*) *Act*, but may nevertheless be liable under common law for negligence and under criminal law, specifically under the *Theft Act*.

However, the management accountant's vital role as coordinator of the efforts of the management team is often recognised and awarded the appropriate status and authority by means of a directorship. In this case his duties and liabilities are considerable.

15. Duties of directors. Directors are essentially trustees and agents of the company whose duties are specified in the rules of the company (Memorandum and Articles of Association, *see* VIII4).

(a) *Trustees*. They are responsible for and must account for the company's money and must refund any which is improperly paid away.

(b) *Agents*. They act as agents when contracting on behalf of the company and incur no personal liability by doing so. But this does not mean that they are allowed a free hand: indeed their duties are spelt out in the Memorandum and

Articles of Association and any breach of these rules renders them personally liable for damages, as do dishonest acts and failure to exercise reasonable skill, bearing in mind the individual's knowledge and experience. In other words, directors have a duty of care towards the company in which they hold office.

16. Management. The *Concise Oxford Dictionary* defines the manager as a "person conducting a business." The vagueness of this definition may hopefully prompt the reader to define his role within his organisation. Apparently not a very difficult task, particularly when the reader–manager has clear terms of references and job specifications. However, it becomes much more difficult to devise a general definition of the manager or management that satisfies all business situations; indeed the whole subject is a source of endless books and articles in management journals. Therefore, at the risk of disagreement let us assume that management is "the exercising of responsibilities in the areas of personnel, resources and finance." This involves the following:

(*a*) Indentification of company objectives, *e.g.* increase in market share in unit or value terms, increase in share price, best possible return on the capital employed in the company, etc. These objectives give direction and purpose to management.

(*b*) Planning strategies or the means of achieving these objectives.

(*c*) Deployment and control of the desired resources, *e.g.* materials and equipment etc., personnel and finance contained in the strategic plans.

(*d*) Reviewing the performance of company operations to see if the company is on course to meet the declared objectives. Clearly clarity of objectives are a pre-requisite for successful management; generally the desired characteristics of objectives are that they should be:

(*i*) Capable of quantification.
(*ii*) Expressable in plain language.
(*iii*) Specific in terms of timing.
(*iv*) Ends in themselves and not means to another end.
(*v*) Capable of revision.

17. Management and the accountant. Figure 2 illustrates the relationships between the financial and management accountants and management itself.

(*a*) *Management.* Management is responsible for the whole of company organisation and its operations. This involves an examination of the firm's environment and consideration of the influencing forces, *e.g.* governmental economic and social policies, technological developments, markets and

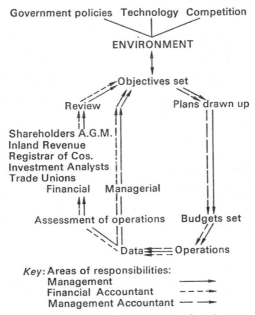

FIG. 2.—Relationships between financial and managerial accountants and management.

competition, for the purpose of establishing objectives for the organisation. The next stage is the drawing-up of plans and budgets for the deployment of resources, personnel and finance to meet the company's goals. Operations are then undertaken and activities controlled according to plan. In due course, performance is analysed by management and interested outside parties, and objectives are reviewed in the light of comment on company performance by shareholders at the company's Annual General Meeting, and by the Inland Revenue, the financial press and the trade unions.

(b) *Financial accountants* are directly responsible for the recording of financial data in accordance with accounting convention and principles and the financial assessment of operations. Company financial performance is reported in the company's published accounts.

(c) *Management accounts.* The management accountant's role of information manager, adviser on financial matters, designer, installer and controller of management systems places him in the centre of the management process. Clearly he advises on objectives and planning, interprets management's plans in the form of accounting budgets, measures performance and controls activities to budgets, and advises management on the viability of company objectives and policies.

PROGRESS TEST 3

1. What are the advantages of forming a joint stock company? (4–5)

2. Explain fully the meaning of "the capital of a company." (6)

3. Compare and contrast the duties and responsibilities of the financial and management accountant. (7–14)

4. "Management should have explicit objectives." Discuss. (16–17)

CHAPTER IV

BASIC ACCOUNTING

DOUBLE ENTRY ACCOUNTING

1. Introduction. The reader has probably already wondered how the accountant records the many hundreds or thousands of business transactions that occur over a trading period. Obviously it must involve a systematic treatment of all transactions; the Profit and Loss Account and Balance Sheet that are drawn up at the conclusion of a trading period to summarise the transactions that have taken place do not magically appear, but are the outcome of a book keeping system that is probably founded on the Italian method of *double entry* already mentioned.

It is important that the businessman and the manager should have a clear understanding of double entry if they are to master basic financial accounting principles. Only then are they in a position to develop skills in interpreting the financial data extracted from an accounting system to answer the following questions at any point in time:

- (*a*) How much is owed by the company or department, and to whom.
- (*b*) How much the company or department owes and to whom.
- (*c*) Whether the company or department is gaining or losing.
- (*d*) Why and in what areas the gains or losses occur.

2. Double entry. Consider the following equation that shows the relationship between company liabilities and assets:

$$\text{Owners' funds} + \text{creditors' funds} = \text{Assets}$$
$$i.e. \text{ Capital} + \text{liabilities} = \text{Assets}$$

This means that the total assets of the company are claimed either by the shareholders or creditors who have supplied either

money, or money's worth. Clearly any increase in capital
causes an equal increase in assets; any reduction in liabilities
causes an equal decrease in assets. In general terms, any
transaction causing a change in any one item in this equation
causes an equal change in either of the other two. Double
entry has been developed to record the twin aspects of such
changes that occur with every business transaction.

The two-fold aspect of double entry can best be appreciated
by way of an example. If Ivor Hogg buys a pint of bitter for
cash, then he *receives value* of beer (debit Beer Account) but
gives *value out* by way of cash (credit Cash Account). From the
publican's point of view the transactions are reversed: *receives
value* (debit Cash Account) and gives *value out* (credit Beer
Account). Thus in summary one debits the account *receiving
value* and credits the account giving *value out*.

3. Rules of debit and credit. The following rules apply:

(*a*) *Debit entries* are:

   (*i*) Increase in assets.
   (*ii*) Decrease in liabilities.
   (*iii*) Decrease in capital.

(*b*) *Credit entries* are:

   (*i*) Decrease in assets.
   (*ii*) Increase in liabilities.
   (*iii*) Increase in capital.

4. Example of double entry transactions.

On 1st January, 1976 Ivor Hogg and others formed a
company, Ivor Hogg & Co., and issued 1,000 shares of £1 for
cash.

   2.1.76   Ivor Hogg & Co. bought goods for resale for £400.
   3.1.76   The company bought a delivery van for £500
             cash.
   4.1.76   It sold goods costing £100 to ZZ Co. for £350 cash.
   5.1.76   It sold goods costing £200 to WW Co. for £400
             on credit.
   8.1.76   It bought goods on credit from TT Co. for £200.
   9.1.76   It paid wages of £30 cash.

IVOR HOGG & CO. LTD.

Share Capital Account

Dr.			Cr.
	£		£
10.1.76 Balance c/d	1,000	1.1.76 Cash	1,000
	1,000		1,000

Cash Account

1.1.76 Share capital	1,000	2.1.76 Purchases	400
4.1.76 Sales	350	3.1.76 Delivery van	500
		9.1.76 Wages	30
		10.1.76 Balance c/d	420
	1,350		1,350

Purchases Account

2.1.76 Cash	400	10.1.76 Trading A/c	600
8.1.76 TT Co.	200		
	600		600

Delivery Van Account

3.1.76 Cash	500	10.1.76 Balance c/d	500
	500		500

Sales Account

10.1.76 Trading A/c	750	4.1.76 Cash	350
		5.1.76 WW Co.	400
	750		750

WW Co. Account

5.1.76 Sales	400	10.1.76 Balance c/d	400
	400		400

TT Co. Account

10.1.76 Balance c/d	200	8.1.76 Purchases	200
	200		200

Wages Account

9.1.76 Cash	30	10.1.76 Profit & Loss A/c	30
	30		30

FIG. 3.—Accounts for the preparation of a Trial Balance for
Ivor Hogg & Co. Ltd.

The reader should now work through the accounts in the above Ivor Hogg Co. Accounts, checking the debit and credit entries for each transaction by means of the appropriate date. Next, to ensure that all these transactions have been correctly recorded, we take out a Trial Balance on 10.1.76. This means

TRIAL BALANCE AT 10.1.76

	Dr £	Cr £
Share capital		1,000
Cash	420	
Purchases	600	
Delivery van	500	
Sales		750
WW Co.	400	
TT Co.		200
Wages	30	
	£1,950	£1,950

Fig. 4.—Trial Balance of Ivor Hogg & Co. Ltd.

totalling each account and comparing the grand totals to make sure that total debits equal total credits.

The final stage is to draw up a Trading and Profit and Loss Account to find out how successful Ivor Hogg & Co. has been over the period. This means that all balances on revenue and expense accounts are transferred on 10.1.76 to the Trading and Profit and Loss Account. At this point a Stock Account is

STOCK ACCOUNT

Dr.   Cr.

10.1.76 Trading A/c   £300 |

Fig. 5.—Stock Account of Ivor Hogg & Co. Ltd.

required for the closing stock of £300 (purchases £600, *less* cost of sales £300); £300 is debited and transferred to the Trading Account which is credited by subtracting from the debit side in order to establish the cost of sales.

The closing balances on the share capital (£1,000), cash (£420), delivery van (£500), creditor (£200) and debtors (£400) become the opening balances for the next trading period.

TRADING AND PROFIT AND LOSS ACCOUNT OF IVOR HOGG & CO. LTD. FOR THE PERIOD ENDED 10.1.76

Purchases	£600	Sales	£750
Less: Stocks at 10.1.76	300		
	——		
Cost of goods sold	300		
Gross profit c/d	450		
	——		——
	750		750
	══		══
Wages	30	Gross profit b/d	450
Net profit	420		
	——		——
	£450		£450
	══		══

FIG. 6.—Trading and Profit and Loss Account of
Ivor Hogg & Co. Ltd.

Thus we see from these accounts that the gross profit was
£450 and net profit £420. Ignoring taxation and dividends
this profit figure is retained and so increases the capital of the
owners to £1,420. The Balance Sheet explains the financial
position of Ivor Hogg & Co. Ltd. at 10.1.76 showing where its
funds have come from and how they have been employed.

BALANCE SHEET OF IVOR HOGG & CO. LTD. AS AT 10.1.76

Capital		*Fixed Assets*	
Shares	£1,000	Delivery van	£500
Profit	420		
	——		
	£1,420	*Current Assets*	
		Stock	300
Current Liabilities		Debtors	400
Trade creditors	200	Cash	420
	——		——
	£1,620		£1,620
	══		══

FIG. 7.—Balance Sheet of Ivor Hogg & Co. Ltd.

ADJUSTMENTS

5. Why adjustments are made. The Trading and Profit and Loss Account and Balance Sheet must represent a "true and fair view" of a company's state of affairs. In order to conform to this company law requirement, close attention must be paid to all prepayments and accruals that relate to the period under consideration. For example, if Ivor Hogg & Co.'s trading year is from 1st January to 31st December and on 1st April a payment is made for £250 for rent for the fifteen month period from 1st January–31st March, then clearly £50 or three months' rent is paid in advance (*see* (*a*) in Fig. 8):

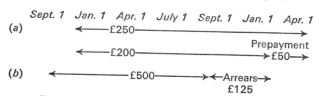

Fig. 8.—Adjustments in the preparation of accounts.

Similarly, if the company pays £500 p.a. interest charges and pays up to September 1st, then Ivor Hogg & Co. Ltd. are in arrears on December 31st when the accounts are drawn up. The value of the interest in arrears is a quarter of £500 = £125 (*see* (*b*) above).

If the adjustments are not made, then the current accounting period will be unfairly burdened with rent expenses that relate to the succeeding period; and the current period will not bear its fair share of interest expenses. Final accounts that fail to reflect these adjustments and thereby the true profit or loss for the period can hardly be described as "true and fair."

6. Nature of adjustments. The following transactions require adjustments to the current period accounts:

(*a*) Prepayments made, *i.e.* payments of expenses that relate to the subsequent period, *e.g.* rent in the above example.

(*b*) Prepayments received, *e.g.* receipts of rent from tenants that are paid in advance.

(c) Payments accrued, *e.g.* value of electricity consumed in the period but not paid.

(d) Receipts accrued, *e.g.* dividend receipts that are overdue.

Items (a) and (d) are assets; (b) and (c) are liabilities of the business, and all should be brought into the Balance Sheet where they are described as follows:

(a) Current asset: payment in advance.
(b) Current liability: income received in advance.
(c) Current liability: accrued expenses.
(d) Current asset: income due but not received.

DEPRECIATION

7. Introduction. Certain assets are owned by companies not for resale but because they are necessary for the production of profits. Machinery, plant and equipment, furniture and fittings and motor vehicles fall into this category. Machinery, plant and equipment are essential in a manufacturing organisation for the production of saleable goods, furniture and fittings provide office staff with facilities that enable them to perform their administrative function and motor vehicles enable company representatives to visit customers and sell goods. However, the existence and use of these assets is not indefinite; they deteriorate and lose value with the passing of time and it is this reduction in value of assets that we term depreciation. It is totally unconnected with the fluctuations in the market price of an asset caused by changes in demand or supply or the vagaries of the market place.

8. Definition. Depreciation is defined as:

The reduction in value of a fixed asset caused by the passing of time, and general wear and tear or obsolescence.

9. Depreciation and the time factor. Some assets become less valuable as time passes. A lease is an obvious example. It is purchased, and provides the tenant with the right of occupancy of premises for a specified period, but is worth less as the expiry date approaches.

10. Depreciation and wear and tear. The usage of assets causes them to deteriorate. For example, machinery or motor

vans deteriorate and become less valuable the harder and
longer they are worked.

11. Depreciation and obsolescence. Motor vehicles as assets
are expected to become obsolete at some future predetermined
time and the asset should be reduced in value every year so
that it stands at zero value when the date of obsolescence
occurs. Alternatively, a manufacturer may be overtaken by
technological progress so that his equipment becomes uneconomic compared with new, more efficient plant.

If a manufacturer can anticipate the effective life of his
capital equipment, then he should spread depreciation over
the asset's expected life.

12. The recording of depreciation. So far we have discussed
the concept of depreciation in terms of the reduction in value
of the asset. This may be shown in the body of the Balance
Sheet or as a note:

Fixed Assets:

Plant and Equipment

Cost		£1,000
Less Depreciation:		
Total depreciation to 31.12.75	£500	
depreciation for 1976	100	
Total depreciation to 31.12.76	£600	£600
		£400

Thus plant costing £1,000 originally has been reduced in
value by a total of £600 so that it stands in the company's
books at £400.

The Plant and Equipment Account would read:

PLANT AND EQUIPMENT ACCOUNT

Dr.		*Cr.*	
1.1.76 Balance b/d	£500	31.12.76 Profit and Loss A/c	£100
		31.12.76 Balance c/d	£400
	£500		£500
1.1.77 Balance b/d	£400		

FIG. 9.—Plant and Equipment Account of Ivor Hogg & Co. Ltd.

However, the point was made in 7 that these assets are employed for the generation of profit and it is surely sensible and equitable to charge these annual reductions in value or costs of deterioration against the profits that result from the use of these assets. If such costs are ignored, then profits are clearly overstated. Furthermore, this act of charging depreciation against profit ensures the identical adjustments to both sides of the Balance Sheet so that they balance. Thus in the above example assets are reduced in value by £100 in 1976, and the corresponding adjustment on the liability side would be:

Profits (say) for 1976	£7,000
Less: Depreciation for 1976	100
Net profit	£6,900

13. The need to provide for depreciation. There is an overwhelming case to be made in favour of providing for depreciation against an asset.

(*a*) The asset generates profit and this profit should bear the cost of the asset over its effective life. If a company that leases equipment offsets the hire charge against profits, then a company actually owning equipment should similarly charge its annual cost against profit. This ensures comparability and a realistic measurement of profits.

(*b*) Depreciation should be provided and the asset reduced in value by that amount so that the Balance Sheet can present a true and fair view of the state of financial affairs. A Balance Sheet that contains an item: *One ten-year-old delivery van*, valued at *cost*: £1,000 and no depreciation provision, can hardly be so described!

(*c*) If no depreciation is provided, then profits will be overstated which, if fully distributed, means that insufficient funds are retained within the organisation to finance their eventual replacement. In other words, the depreciation charge directly reduces the amount of profit available for distributing to the shareholders or owners of the business and so retains cash or money's worth within the organisation. Therefore at the end of the life of the asset, funds equal to the cost of the asset are available within the firm with which to buy a replacement asset.

14. Depreciation and cash flow. A cash flow occurs when cash including cheques are received by a business from an outside party and when similar payments are made by the business to other companies or individuals. Depreciation (a cost) is not paid to persons outside the business and therefore is not a cash outflow. It is not normally paid into a special reserve or account but is retained for general capital expenditure on materials, work in progress, stocks or even additional fixed assets. This last point is important for a company would do well to use depreciation in this way when it can earn a satisfactory return on capital rather than to create a pool of cash that earns little or no return, *i.e.* a company could use its cash pool to finance additional trade if the organisation can earn 20 per cent return on its capital compared with say 10 per cent that banks pay on cash deposits.

15. Depreciation: problem. Many managers who have no training in accountancy find depreciation a difficult concept to grasp. However, a simple example at this stage may help to clarify this very complex subject and consolidate the foregoing comments.

EXAMPLE

Eddie sets up in the self-drive car hire business when he buys a motor car for £1,900 which he estimates has an operational life of ten years. At the end of his first year's business his total income and expenditure is as follows:

Receipts		*Payments*	
Hire revenue	£2,500	Petrol	£300
		Oil	10
		Insurance	80
		Tax	25
		Service and repairs	60
	£2,500		£475

Eddie has no accountant to advise him and in fact uses his personal bank account for both domestic and business transactions. All business receipts are deposited and all payments made by cheque.

Maggie, his wife, analyses the bank statement and is keen to spend the profits of £2,025 on a round-the-world trip for herself and her mother. Eddie is keen that they should go, but doubts whether his real profit is £2,025. Furthermore, he has not drawn any salary.

(*a*) Eddie's bank account has received a net amount of £2,025 but his net profit figure is only £1,835. Why? (*see* **13**).

(*b*) Assuming that Eddie is satisfied with £1,500 as his annual wage, then his profit is £1,835 − £1,500 = £335 which yields a return on investment of 17·6 per cent (£335 ÷ £1,900 × 100). How should he use the profit if bank deposit rates and building society rates are 10·5 per cent and hire purchase interest is 13 per cent (*i.e.* the true rate)?

(*c*) Is the total depreciation provision over the ten years likely to be sufficient for the replacement of the vehicle? If not, why not? (*see* IX, **7**).

NOTE: (*b*) requires some additional comment. If Eddie wishes to maximise his profit then his best policy would be to use the profit of £335 as a down payment for the purchase of a second car because the return on the investment is much higher than bank deposit interest and exceeds the cost of the H.P. finance. However, he still has £190 in his account representing depreciation (*see* (*a*)), and rather than invest the money at bank deposit rate for the ten years, at the end of which he will need the money to replace the car, he can use it more profitably by putting it towards the down payment on a second car. This is exactly what companies do with depreciation provisions. They do not usually invest it in a special *Depreciation Bank Account* but spend it on new materials, equipment, plant, expenses, etc. because it is a cheap source of funds and generates a higher return through profits on company sales than bank deposits or endowment policies.

16. Methods of providing for depreciation. The two methods of providing for depreciation that are most commonly used are:

(*a*) Straight line method.
(*b*) Reducing balance method.

17. Straight line method. In order to apply this method, one requires the following information:

(*a*) The original cost of the asset.
(*b*) The anticipated life of the asset.
(*c*) The estimated scrap value of the asset.

Thus if Basset Company buys a mechanical guillotine for

£900 and estimates its effective life to be six years when its scrap value is probably £100, then depreciation is calculated as follows:

$$\text{Annual depreciation charge} = \frac{\text{original cost} - \text{scrap value}}{\text{life of the asset}}$$

$$= \frac{£900 - £100}{6}$$

$$= \frac{£800}{6}$$

$$= £133\text{·}3$$

This annual depreciation charge is credited to the Asset Account (thereby reducing its value at the end of year one to £766·7) and debited to the Profit and Loss Account (*see* VII). Alternatively, the depreciation charge is debited to the Profit and Loss Account and credited to *Provision for Depreciation Account* and the balance subtracted from the original cost of the asset on the Balance Sheet.

At the end of the sixth year, the total depreciation figure is £133·3 × 6 = £799·8 (£800). This figure has been charged to Profit and Loss by six instalments of £133·3 and the balance standing in the Asset Account and Balance Sheet is £100 (the scrap value).

The name of this method is derived from the shape of the depreciation line in Fig. 10.

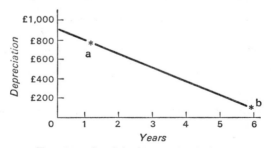

FIG. 10.—Straight line depreciation.

(*a*) Depreciation of £133·3 in year one means that the written-down value is then £766·7, the amount still to be depreciated.
(*b*) At the end of six years the depreciated net cost of the machine (£800) has been recovered through depreciation so that its written-down value matches its scrap value.

18. Reducing balance method. The same information is required as for the straight line method. Then a percentage figure is calculated that reduces the value of the asset to its expected scrap value over its effective life. This percentage figure is then written off the diminishing value of the asset.

19. Reducing balance method: example. Using the same details as in 17 and a 25 per cent depreciation figure (simply to illustrate the procedure) the written down value of the asset will appear as follows:

Year 1	Original cost of guillotine	£900
	Less: 25% depreciation	225
Year 2	Written down value	675
	Less: 25% depreciation	168
Year 3	Written down value	507
	Less: 25% depreciation	126
Year 4	Written down value	381
	Less: 25% depreciation	95
Year 5	Written down value	286
	Less: 25% depreciation	71
Year 6	Written down value	215
	Less: 25% depreciation	54
	Written down value at end of Year 6	161

Obviously the written-down value will not equal the scrap value at the end of the sixth year: this means that 25 per cent is too low. The correct figure is obtained by formula.

20. Formula to calculate the percentage. The formula to calculate the percentage by which to depreciate an asset by the reducing balance method is:

$$r = 1 - \sqrt[n]{S/C}$$

NOTE: S must have a significant value.

where: r = the desired percentage
n = anticipated life of the asset
S = residual value
C = cost of the asset

21. Exercise. Using the formula in **20**, calculate the correct percentage depreciation figure and then rework the depreciation statement contained in **19** to confirm that the written down value of the guillotine at the sixth year equals its residual value (confirm that r = 30·6 per cent).

22. Advantages of the reducing balance method. The following advantages are claimed:

(*a*) Assets initially fall rapidly in value and the initial depreciation charge is similarly high.

(*b*) The efficiency of assets decreases over time: depreciation also decreases.

(*c*) The reducing balance never reaches zero so that the same charge is always made against profit. This is realistic while the company uses the asset. The straight line method however, completely writes off the asset so that the depreciation charge can be zero while the asset is still employed.

PROGRESS TEST 4

1. What are the merits of a "double entry accounting system"? (1–2)

2. What adjustments are made in preparing final accounts and why are these adjustments necessary? (5–6)

3. Define "depreciation" and explain the need to provide for depreciation. (7–13)

4. Compare and contrast the straight line and reducing balance methods of providing for depreciation. (16–22)

CHAPTER V

COSTS: WHAT ARE THEY REALLY?

INTRODUCTION

1. We all know what costs are. Every reader knows what
costs are from personal experience. They are expenses that
stop one from enjoying oneself! But expenses of what? They
may be the high costs of taking one's car abroad in August or
the comparatively low cost of petrol prior to autumn 1973.
The economist explains all costs as being the price for using
scarce factors of production which he classifies as land, labour,
capital and enterprise. All require payment for the use of their
factor services in the form of rent, wages and salaries, interest
and profit respectively, and their relative scarcity, or the
demand for those commodities in relation to available supply,
determines their cost. Cross-channel fares are high because of
the relative scarcity of shipping facilities; petrol, originally
inexpensive because of the availability of relatively large
supplies, became very costly once supplies were restricted.

This economist's definition and classification, although correct, does not consider the character of costs and so we must
look further for alternatives that describe their behaviour.

2. Problem. Ivor, an impecunious motorist, keeps a car log
in which he records all motoring expenses. It shows that his
average yearly mileage is 10,000 miles and his expenses to be
as follows:

(*i*)	Petrol	£170·00
(*ii*)	Oil	10·00
(*iii*)	Service	20·00
(*iv*)	Repairs	40·00
(*v*)	Insurance	40·00
(*vi*)	Road fund licence	25·00
(*vii*)	Garage rent for year paid 1st Jan.	50·00
(*viii*)	Depreciation	100·00

Total:	£455·00, *or* 4·5p/mile

Ivor's wife wishes to visit her mother who lives fifty miles away and asks Ivor to take her by car. Ivor is keen that she should go but since she cannot drive explains that he can't honestly afford the cost of motoring there and back. In fact, he claims it will cost £4·50 (4·5p × 100 miles). His wife's reply is, "Rubbish." Who is correct?

The basic problem here is that these costs have different characteristics. Some have already been paid and others are incurred only if the journey is made, so that if we examine them individually we find that:

(*i*) Petrol costs are incurred in direct proportion to the number of miles travelled;

(*ii*) similarly oil costs.

(*iii*) Services and

(*iv*) repairs are related to mileage;

(*v*) insurance is paid in advance, and is independent of the number of miles Ivor does in a year.

(*vi*) Road fund licence is also independent of mileage;

(*vii*) garage rent has been paid and does not vary with mileage;

(*viii*) depreciation represents the loss in value of the car over the year. Two factors affecting depreciation are the car's mileage and its age; the latter is the more important factor.

In summary, these costs may be conveniently classified according to how they behave:

(*a*) Variable costs which vary directly with mileage:

    (*i*) Petrol.
    (*ii*) Oil.
    (*iii*) Service.
    (*iv*) Repairs.

(*b*) Semi-variable costs which vary with mileage, but not in direct proportion:

    (*v*) Depreciation. Time, not mileage is the main determinant of car depreciation.

(*c*) Fixed costs are constant and unaffected by mileage:

    (*vi*) Insurance.
    (*vii*) Road fund licence.
    (*viii*) Garage rent.

Thus the cost of the journey consists of the variable costs

and the variable part of the semi-variable cost (let us assume this is 25 per cent).

Cost per mile = petrol + oil + service + repairs + 25% of depreciation

Cost per mile = 1·7p + 0·1p + 0·2p + 0·4p + 25% of 1p
= 2·65p

Cost of the journey = 2·65p × 100
= £2·65

3. How many costs are there? Further examination of this apparently simple example will identify yet more ways of looking at costs. For example:

(a) *The cost of motoring.* This is the total cost of owning and using the car. Here it is £455 per year. Ivor may feel that he cannot afford to go on paying the total cost of motoring of £455 each year. But will he save £455 each year if he sells his car? Can he avoid all costs if he keeps it in the garage or sells it now part way through the year? Obviously not.

(b) *User cost.* He will certainly not incur the costs of using the car as opposed to leaving it idle.

(c) *Marginal or incremental costs.* These are the additional costs of a small increase in the variable unit. In this example the marginal = incremental = variable cost is the cost of an additional mile travelled, or the 100-mile journey. These can be avoided by not using the car.

(d) *Sunk costs.* However, Ivor cannot avoid costs that are irreversible. He has paid the garage rent and is not entitled to a rebate if he cancels the lease. Nor can he get back the expired portion of the insurance and road fund licence.

(e) *Opportunity cost.* This is the economist's concept that may be usefully applied to any situation where a choice is made between alternatives. It is defined as the opportunity foregone or sacrifice involved in making a choice. Thus the opportunity cost of Ivor running his own car is the sacrifice involved in not investing the capital; if he sold his car he would benefit from the investment of the proceeds on which he could earn perhaps interest of 10 per cent per annum, *less*, of course, the cost of using public transport.

Furthermore the concept is capable of further extension:

the opportunity cost of the 100-mile journey may be expressed as the £2·65 saved by not going: alternatively the opportunity cost of not driving is the cost of using the train.

(*f*) *Standard cost.* Ivor, in addition to his other talents, is a qualified mechanic and keeps his car permanently tuned for peak efficiency. Thus the above cost schedule (*see* 2) becomes a set of standard costs showing what the various costs of motoring ought to be for maximum operating efficiency over 10,000 miles. Ivor, by comparing his actual running costs with these predetermined costs, can ensure that his car is operating efficiently.

(*g*) *Historical costs.* These are the costs of transactions at the time they are made. Thus Ivor's car cost £1,500 in 1971, and four new tyres were fitted in 1973 at a total cost of £35. Both illustrate historical original costs.

(*h*) *Replacement costs.* This is the current or expected cost of replacing something. Ivor's car may cost £1,800 to replace in 1974 with a similar model, compared with its historical cost of £1,500.

Costs at first sight present a bewildering array of concepts and terms. Indeed, the terminology is not always consistent but varies between books on costing; sometimes reference is made to indirect costs or overheads, standard costs or planned costs, marginal cost or variable cost, etc. Nevertheless, it is hoped that the reader has drawn one important conclusion from the above example, that costs are different according to the set of circumstances under examination and that the term "cost" without qualification is to be deprecated. Clearly, an understanding of the nature of the principle cost concepts is essential if the reader is to proceed with confidence to the analysis of costing that follows.

COST CURVES

4. Cost and output. The graphs that follow show in visual form the general relationships between average and total costs and output.

5. Fixed costs and output. Fixed costs are by definition constant, regardless of a firm's level of activity. Thus if a manufacturer has fixed costs of £50,000 representing management's salaries, rent, rates and insurance, etc., they are constant at £50,000 whether one unit or 100,000 units of output are produced.

However, fixed costs per unit of output or average fixed costs (fixed costs ÷ output) vary according to output. The average fixed cost for one unit of output is obviously £50,000; as output increases, average fixed costs fall because the numerator in the fraction is spread over a larger output, so that for 100,000 units it is only 50p. These relationships between fixed costs and output are illustrated in Figs. 11 and 12.

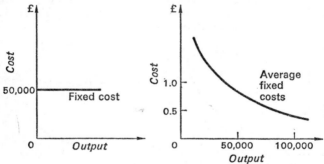

FIG. 11.—Total fixed cost.

FIG. 12.—Average fixed costs. This curve is a rectangular hyperbola; every cost/output combination shown by the curve produces a constant total fixed cost of £50,000.

6. Variable cost and output. All organisations using factors of production whose employment can be varied, *e.g.* labour in combination with fixed factors such as a piece of land or a factory, would experience the effects of the law of non-proportional returns if they attempted to expand output from zero to full capacity by taking on additional units of the variable factor. Initially a single man employed in the factory would make a negligible impact on output, a second might help slightly, a third, fourth, fifth and so on would each contribute more to total output than the preceding operative through the operation of the law of increasing returns. Therefore cost/unit of output or average variable cost would be high at the outset and fall gradually until it reaches a minimum where there is an ideal match between the number of men and the factory facilities. However, as additional men are employed to expand output further, overmanning occurs so that each additional worker adds less to total output than the previous man. Consequently, output per man falls through the law of decreasing returns causing average variable costs to rise. This is illustrated in Fig. 14.

Fig. 13 illustrates the relationship between total variable costs and output. These costs rise steeply at first, then less steeply when the above economies of production are enjoyed. Finally, as output approaches full capacity, they rise very steeply again because diseconomies in production mean that wages increase at a faster rate than output.

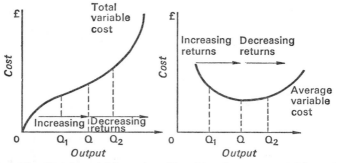

FIG. 13.—Total variable cost.   FIG. 14.—Average variable cost.

7. Total costs and output. Total costs consist of variable cost plus fixed costs (*i*). This may be expressed in terms of average costs (*ii*).

(*i*) TC = VC + FC
(*ii*) ATC = AVC + AFC

Thus we can establish the general shape of the total cost (TC) curve and average total cost (ATC) curve by the summation of the curves for variable and fixed costs. This is illustrated by Figs. 15 and 16.

8. Cost curves over the operational range. So far we have examined the relationships between costs and output over the entire range of output, *i.e.* from zero to full capacity. However,

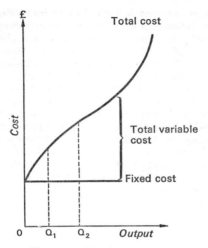

FIG. 15.—Total cost curve.

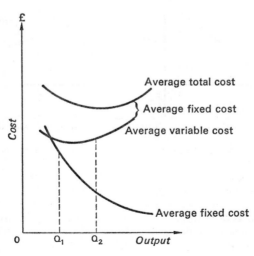

FIG. 16.—Average total cost curve.

in practice, management is immediately interested only in the cost/output relationship over its operational range of production, *e.g.* Q_1-Q_2 in Figures 15 to 16, where the cost curves are virtually straight lines because of near-constant returns to the variable factors. Therefore if we redraw these cost curves and expand the scale on the horizontal axis covering the appropriate range of activity, we produce graphs (Figs. 17 and 18) that relate fixed, variable and total costs to the operational range of activity. In general terms, they simplify the cost/volume relationship and provide a visual presentation which is useful to managers and management accountants in decision making within the areas of production and cost control. However, this does not imply that these earlier graphs are irrelevant to managers, indeed they can play an important role in showing management what would happen to costs if output were to contract or expand significantly.

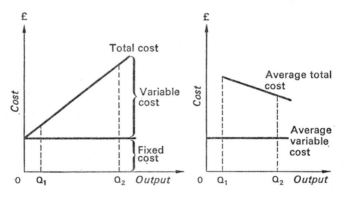

FIG. 17.—Total cost curve.   FIG. 18.—Average cost curve.

BASIC COSTING

9. Objects of costing. Costing, described as the implementation and operation of a system to provide cost data for management information, has the following objects:

(*a*) To provide managers with information they require

to solve the economic problem, *i.e.* to make the most effective use of the limited resources they have at their disposal. In practical terms this means cost control:

    (*i*) Identifying every source of cost.
    (*ii*) Assigning responsibility of these costs to managers.
    (*iii*) Monitoring costs.
    (*iv*) Controlling costs to a predetermined plan.

  (*b*) To supply data on which to base policy.
  (*c*) To provide cost estimates of future operations.

10. Advantages of costing. There is no single costing system applicable to every business situation; the complexity and diversity of business means that each firm needs a costing system to meet its own requirements. However, a comprehensive tailor-made system can yield the following benefits:

  (*a*) It identifies profitable operations and activities.
  (*b*) It identifies relative profitabilities between different operations and activities.
  (*c*) It identifies areas of waste or loss.
  (*d*) It provides a basis for cost reduction exercises.
  (*e*) It provides information useful in setting selling prices, *e.g.* tenders.
  (*f*) It enables management to plan and control activities.

11. Industrial classification of costs. In the company's Profit and Loss Account, costs are classified by the type of cost, *e.g.* selling and distribution costs and administration costs, etc. (*see* X and XI) but in costing statements used by industrial organisations they are classified differently, *i.e.* by jobs, and departments, etc.

  (*a*) *Direct costs or prime costs.* These are costs that can be directly identified with specific units of output. In particular they are:

    (*i*) Materials, *e.g.* raw materials contained in the product.
    (*ii*) Wages,   *e.g.* wages of machine operators who make the product.
    (*iii*) Expenses, *e.g.* power used to make the product.

(*b*) *Indirect costs or overheads*. These costs are incurred for the whole organisation or department, and cannot be identified with specific units of output:

  (*i*) Manufacturing overheads, *e.g.* factory rent.
  (*ii*) Administration overheads, *e.g.* audit fees.
  (*iii*) Selling and distribution overheads, *e.g.* sales director's salary.

These direct and indirect costs are incurred throughout the production process, and to describe and quantify the costs incurred at a certain stage in this process, the following terms and definitions are generally used:

  (*c*) Prime or original or direct cost (*see* (*a*)).
  (*d*) Manufacturing or production or works or factory costs
      = (*c*) + manufacturing indirect costs.
  (*e*) Cost of production or gross cost
      = (*d*) + administration indirect costs.
  (*f*) Cost of sales
      = (*e*) + selling and distribution indirect costs.
  (*g*) Selling price
      = (*f*) + profit (or − a loss).

This last point (*g*) should be particularly noted.

EXAMPLE:

Materials	£1,000
Wages	4,000
Power	500
(*c*) Prime cost	5,500
Manufacturing overheads	600
(*d*) Factory cost	6,100
Administration overheads	400
(*e*) Cost of Production	6,500
Selling and distribution overheads	300
(*f*) Cost of sales	6,800
Profit	1,000
(*g*) Selling price	£7,800

12. Collecting costing data. Costs are incurred at every stage of the production process directly by payment for materials and individuals and indirectly by payments for benefits received from service departments. Clearly it is important for management to know precisely the type and amount of costs wherever incurred. To this end, cost centres or *cost collection points* are established, and all costs incurred by, or that relate to specific cost centres are charged to the appropriate cost collection point. These cost centres may be:

(a) A location, *e.g.* a department, sales region, warehouse.
(b) A piece of equipment, *e.g.* a forge, hydraulic press, motor van.
(c) A person, *e.g.* sales manager.
(d) A group of these.

Thus a motor van cost centre will be charged with the expenses that it incurs or relate to it, *e.g.* depreciation, petrol and oil, repairs and service, road tax, etc.

13. Advantages of cost centre costing. The advantages of charging costs to specific cost centres are:

(a) It forms a sound foundation for a costing system.
(b) It enables managers to compare the total cost of operating the cost centre with the benefit it provides, *e.g.* the motor van cost centre may show that £2,000 per year is spent on the vehicle, yet it is directly responsible for delivering finished goods worth, say, £80,000 per year quickly and reliably. Management may decide that the advantage of prompt delivery outweighs the excess cost of operating the vehicle over alternative methods of dispatch, *e.g.* parcel post.

14. Cost units. In addition costs may be expressed in terms of units of output or service:

(a) Units of output, *e.g.* barrels of beer, cubic metres of sand, a job.
(b) Units of service, *e.g.* 1,000 seat miles, kilowatt-hours.

ALLOCATION OF OVERHEADS

15. Total costs. Most businesses operate on a full cost or total cost basis. This means that a typical product's costing analysis will look something like this:

Product X

Direct costs	Materials	£1,000
	Labour	2,000
	Power	100
		3,100
Indirect costs	Administration	200
	Selling and distribution	800
Total costs		4,100
	+ Profit 20%	820
Selling price		£4,920

FIG. 19.—Typical product costing analysis.

Administration, selling and distribution overheads represent the costs of non-revenue producing departments and obviously must be borne by departments that do earn revenue. Furthermore, these costs must be absorbed by specific units of output. In the above example, there is no difficulty if only one unit of product X is made. But there is a problem if there is more than one product and several units of each are made.

Theoretically there is no problem. For reasons of equity each unit should bear its fair share of overheads, *i.e.* in proportion to the benefits or services each receives from the administration and selling and distribution departments. But in practice there is often a real difficulty in identifying and measuring the real benefit or service. The solution may be to apportion by means of formula.

16. Apportionment procedure. The procedure for apportioning indirect expenses is as follows:

(*a*) The total cost of expenses at each service cost centre is established.

(b) Expenses that can be charged directly to individual production cost centres for service benefits are allocated.

(c) A formula is devised to apportion the balance of unapportioned costs. This may be on the basis of floor area for rent and rates or number of employees for administration costs.

(d) Indirect costs of the production cost centres are added on giving total overheads to be allocated among products passing through the production department.

(e) An equitable basis is used whereby units of goods passing through departments absorb these overheads, e.g. if a department is highly labour intensive then the basis for absorbing overheads may be:

$$\text{Labour hour rate}: \frac{\text{overheads}}{\text{direct labour hours}}$$

Thus if total overheads for this department are £20,000, and anticipated labour hours are 15,000, then the charge would be £1·33 per labour hour.

Thus, job no. 101:	
Materials	£6·00
Labour 15 hours @ 50p	7·50
Prime cost	13·50
Overhead 15 hours @ £1·33	19·95
Total cost	£33·45

TYPES OF COSTING SYSTEMS

17. Job costing. A plumber ought to know the profit or loss on each job: hence a job costing system is used to calculate the cost of individual jobs or contracts. Batch costing is a variant. Here, as in an engineering works, a number of items, making up one order, pass through the conversion process as a batch. In both cases, job sheets will be made out on which are recorded all expenses that specifically relate to the job or batch.

18. Process costing. This system is employed where the product passes through stages or processes which make it impossible to identify any one unit of product. For example, one cannot specify the exact cost attributable to one gallon of petrol or kilo of chemical or flour. In fact, the cost of an individual order can only be calculated by reference to the cost per unit passing through the process over a period of time.

19. Standard costing. This is a means whereby predetermined costs for a unit of output, process or operation (executed efficiently) are compared with actual costs (*i.e.* comparing actual performance with what it ought to have been). It is particularly important as a control technique since comparison between planned and actual performance throws up deviations or "variances" which can be investigated by management.

20. Limitations of historical costing. In many businesses actual costs incurred in one period are used as a standard for subsequent periods. Such comparisons may have some use in highlighting areas for investigation but this system has distinct limitations because in the real world companies operate in a dynamic environment. Historical cost comparisons are only valid in a static situation:

(*a*) The state of the market may have changed.

(*b*) Direct costs may be different because of changes in wage rates, or inflation in commodity markets.

(*c*) Indirect costs may be different because of inflation, *i.e.* all overheads may cost more.

(*d*) Production standards may be different because of new production techniques or productivity agreements.

Therefore, historical costing, *i.e.* what has happened in terms of cost, is of limited value in cost control: standard costing, *i.e.* what ought to happen in terms of future costs, is clearly preferable.

21. Setting a standard cost. In order to establish a standard cost, management uses past costing data updated in the light of current or expected conditions to arrive at a planned cost which is reasonably expected to apply in the future.

The standard cost of an article would be calculated on the following lines. Firstly the product is analysed into its component parts or operations. Secondly an allowed time for each operation is calculated by work study methods, and direct costs applied. Thirdly, overheads are charged by an agreed formula. Finally, these costs are added together to find the standard cost of the article.

Materials
5 kilos of alloy @ £3·00/kilo		=	£15·00
1 packing case @ £1·50		=	1·50

Labour
Lathe operator 2 hours @ £1·00/hr		=	2·00
Spot welder ½ hour @ £1·50/hr		=	0·75
Metal polisher 1 hour @ £1·00/hr		=	1·00

Overheads
3½ hours @ 50p/hr		=	1·75

Standard cost/unit		£22·00

Where a standard costing system is already in existence, the procedure is straightforward. All one has to do is to add up the standard costs of the constituent cost units involved in the production of the article.

22. Marginal costing. Marginal costing is based on the concept of marginal cost originally developed by economists who define it as the incremental cost of one additional unit of output. A sound appreciation of the distinction between fixed and variable costs and their effect on total cost and profit resulting from changes in output is essential for a thorough understanding of marginal costing.

Fixed costs are by definition incurred irrespective of the volume of output and sales; variable costs are proportional to output. If sales revenue exceeds variable cost (marginal cost) then a contribution is made towards a fund that in total should cover fixed costs. Its advantage is that it allows greater flexibility in pricing policy than a full cost pricing system (*see* 15).

Assume fixed costs are £25,000 and that two products A and B are made with variable costs of £6 and £7 respectively. They sell for £12 and £15; output and sales are 5,000 and 4,000 respectively. Clearly the extra cost of producing a marginal unit, *i.e.* 5,001 of A and 4,001 of B is the variable cost (£6 and £7). In other words, marginal cost means variable cost.

	A		B		Total
Sales	5,000 @ £12	£60,000	4,000 @ £15	£60,000	120,000
Variable costs	5,000 @ £6	30,000	4,000 @ £7	28,000	58,000
Contribution		30,000		32,000	62,000
Contribution of one extra unit		6		8	14
Total contributions from the sale of 5,001 units		30,006	(4,001 units)	32,008	62,014

$$\text{Profit} = \text{Total contributions} - \text{fixed costs}$$
$$£37,014 = £62,014 - £25,000$$

The above example illustrates the principle of marginal
costing. In particular, fixed costs are not allocated to products
as in total costing (*see* **15**) but are covered by a fund of contributions made by selling above variable costs. The additional
contribution made by the sale of an additional unit results in
a clear profit of an identical amount because fixed costs do not
increase with sales and are already fully covered at these levels
of sales. Marginal costing is examined in greater detail in
Chapter XI.

PROGRESS TEST 5

1. Explain the difference between fixed and variable costs.
(1–3)
2. How does the law of non-proportional returns affect costs?
(4–8)
3. Identify and explain the advantages of costing. **(9–11)**
4. Explain the following terms:
   (*a*) cost centres;
   (*b*) cost units;
   (*c*) prime costs;
   (*d*) job costing;
   (*e*) standard costing. **(12–20)**

5. "Contribution = sales price less marginal cost." Explain.
(22)

CHAPTER VI

THE BALANCE SHEET

INTRODUCTION

In Chapters I and II we examined the nature of money, the lubricant of the modern exchange system and how business obtains these funds to finance its trade. Chapters III and IV dealt with how business records the various uses to which this money is put by means of its accounting system and Chapter V explained the nature of costs and the way money is spent on business transactions.

In this chapter we now draw together these threads to see at any one point in time how much money, in total and in its various forms, a firm possesses after it has incurred these costs. We do this and thereby show the financial state of the business by summarising the balances in the company's books by means of a Balance Sheet.

1. The Balance Sheet. A Balance Sheet is a statement, not an account, that records the financial position of a company at one moment in time. The accountant who prepares this statement is in effect *taking a snapshot* of the company which if taken earlier or later would have produced a different financial statement.

It does not, as is widely believed, explain how successfully the company has fared over the year (this is the function of the Profit and Loss Account) but gives a "true and fair view" (*see* VIII) of the company's financial position in the form of the equation outlined in 2.

2. Source of funds = use of funds. The Balance Sheet is essentially a source and use of funds statement, *i.e.* it shows in detail where the company's funds have come from and how these funds have been employed.

79

3. Example of a simple Balance Sheet. Imagine that an individual, Ivor Hogg, tots up his possessions in the form of the following financial statement.

POSSESSIONS (ASSETS) OWNED BY IVOR HOGG AT 31.12.76

House	£20,000
Household contents	500
Colour TV	200
Car	2,000
Cash	1
	£22,701

Fig. 20.—Assets of Ivor Hogg Esq.

This list of assets is an expansion of the second part of the equation in **2** (*i.e.* use of funds), showing how Ivor has spent money coming into his possession. However, if the statement is to show a "true and fair view" of his financial position then it must be extended to indicate the various claims that individuals and organisations have on him (*i.e.* his liabilities). This is done by listing his sources of funds as at 31.12.76.

1. Mortgage on house	£12,000
2. H.P. on car	1,500
3. Loan from uncle (Bank Manager)	5,000
4. Bank loan on furniture	400
5. Bank overdraft	3,000
Total funds from external sources	21,900

If this is the total of funds from external sources then Ivor must have supplied the balance of funds himself to finance his assets, *i.e.* £801.

Thus applying and expanding the equation from **2** we have:

Total sources of funds = Total use of funds
£22,701 = £22,701
or Owners funds + creditors = Assets
£801 + £21,900 = £22,701
or Owners funds = Assets − creditors
£801 = £22,701 − £21,900

4. The water tank analogy. The following analogy is a simple yet effective way of explaining the relationship between assets and liabilities. It also introduces the concept of *funds flow*.

Imagine that £10K worth of money (like water) from a variety of sources is poured into a company's cash tank (*see* Fig. 21). Assuming that the tank is empty at the start it now contains £10K. However, the purpose of business is not simply to hold funds; in order to meet its objectives, management will decide by means of investment appraisal how much of these funds to release for the purchase of permanent or fixed assets. The diagram shows that £5K has been drawn off into a fixed assets tank; £2K has been put into land, £2K into plant and machinery and £1K into equipment.

Similarly money is spent (and the exact amounts metered by the Profit and Loss Account) on raw materials; overheads and labour are employed to convert the materials into stocks of finished goods, *e.g.*:

Cost of raw materials	£1,500
Wages	2,000
Power, light and heat	500
Cost of finished goods	£4,000

Extending the analogy further, we see that the current asset tank that contains temporary cash-generating assets has a sales pump attached that pumps sales revenue up into the main tank, so becoming an additional source of funds.

A careful examination of the diagram reveals that total sources of funds (£10K) must equal total uses (£10K) (*i.e.* liabilities = assets) and that these are kept in balance by means of the sales pump.

Thus total sources of finance are:

Shareholders	£5K
Bank	3
Creditors	2

£10K which equals the use of funds

Fixed assets

Land	£2K	
Plant and machinery	2	
Equipment	1	
	—	£5K

Current assets

Stocks of finished goods	4K	
Cash (unused)	1	
	—	£5K

£10K

To complete the analogy, there are two outlets to be considered; one is corporation tax that is automatically syphoned off as profits are made, and the other is the dividend paid to shareholders on the recommendation of the directors. Drawing up the Balance Sheet is simplicity itself in this example. The accountant reads off the levels on a dipstick inserted into each of the tanks showing the disposition of funds entering the system.

5. Tank analogy problem. The reader should test his understanding of the analogy by answering the following question (ignore depreciation).

If there are no additional sources of funds and no withdrawals from the system, will the total funds contained within the system decrease, increase or remain the same if:

(*a*) Finished goods are sold at exactly cost of production (*i.e.* at break-even)?

(*b*) Finished goods are sold above cost of production (*i.e.* for a profit)?

(*c*) Finished goods are sold below cost of production (*i.e.* at a loss)?

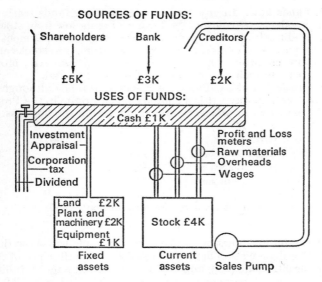

FIG. 21.—The water tank analogy.

Check that your answers read: (*a*) remain the same, (*b*) increase, and (*c*) decrease.

6. Capital and revenue expenditure. It is important to distinguish and record separately company expenditure that is made for revenue and capital purposes, and the distinction must be clearly understood at the outset. Some monies are spent on items that are required as a means to the end of producing profit, *i.e.* additions, extensions to or improvements to assets, *e.g.* plant and machinery which are used to process materials into saleable goods. Such expenditure is capital and is a Balance Sheet item classified under fixed assets.

Other expenditure that is short-term by comparison and is directly related to the conversion process is revenue, and is charged in the Profit and Loss Account against profit. Put another way, capital expenditure results in or is due to the acquisition of an asset. Revenue expenditures are normal trading expenses.

7. Funds flow. In any trading organisation, funds (cash or its equivalent) are continually flowing. Funds flow from stocks into credit sales (debtors); debtors into cash when payment is made; purchases of stocks by credit (creditors) into stocks and cash into creditors, when payment is made. Similarly, profit may increase cash or other items of working capital.

Depreciation of fixed assets is a source of funds although it is not a cash outlay. It is a charge against profits in the Profit and Loss Account and so retains profit within the business.

Gross profit		£1,000
Less: Overheads	£100	
Wages	£300	
Depreciation	£200	600
Net profit available for distribution		£400

A careful examination of the above example will show that the £200 depreciation figure is a retention of profit since of the total profits made (£1,000), only overheads and wages totalling £400 represent payments to outsiders. The balance £600 is retained (*i.e.* net profit £400 + depreciation £200).

8. Problem. Before progressing any further with Balance Sheet analysis, it is vital that the reader has a sound grasp of the basic structure of the Balance Sheet. For this purpose, typical Balance Sheet items are given below, and the reader should ask himself whether each item is a source or a use of funds, and reassemble them correctly in the accompanying *pro forma* Balance Sheet.

1. Overdraft.
2. Preference shares.
3. Motor vehicles.
4. Land.
5. Stocks of finished goods.
6. Retained profits.
7. Corporation tax due but not paid.
8. Debtors.
9. Creditors.
10. Furniture and fittings.
11. Work in progress.
12. Ordinary shares.
13. Cash in hand.
14. Dividends due but not paid.
15. Two year loan from I.C.F.C.
16. Plant and machinery.
17. Goodwill.

BALANCE SHEET OF X LIMITED AT 31.12.76

Liabilities (Sources)	*Assets* (Uses)
Long-term	Fixed assets
Medium-term	Current assets
Short-term	
£	£

FIG. 22.—Balance sheet of X Co. Ltd.

NOTES:

1. Short-term source that becomes payable within one year.
2. Long-term or permanent source.
3. Fixed asset; a use to which money has been invested to generate present and future sales.
4. As 3.
5. Current asset: a use of funds that generates sales revenue in the short term.
6. Long-term source of funds generated internally.
7. Short-term source of funds. It really belongs to the Inland Revenue and so is a source of short-term finance until it is actually paid.
8. Current asset. Obviously a use of funds since these customers have received goods but have not paid.
9. Short-term source. Trade suppliers have supplied money's worth.
10. As 3.
11. Current asset: represents money tied up in semi-finished goods.
12. As 2.
13. Current asset.
14. As 7.
15. Medium-term source of funds.
16. As 3.
17. This arises when a company takes over another and is equal to the premium paid by the purchaser over and above the actual value shown by the vendors' Balance Sheet. There are many reasons why a purchaser may pay a price in excess of the current value but generally he feels that the current value does not reflect the true earning potential. The amount of premium (goodwill) paid will naturally

depend on the anticipated value of future earnings. The purchasing company will combine the two Balance Sheets and show the goodwill figure as a fixed asset or as a separate item under "intangible asset," and should be prudent enough to write it off fairly quickly on the grounds that goodwill could disappear overnight if the economy suffers a recession or if customers turn to competitors. Traditionally, "conservatism" has been the rule for company accounts.

EXAMPLE: Draw up a Balance Sheet for G. Smith, a wholesale merchant, from the following information.

Bank overdraft	£100
Cash in hand	90
Furniture and fittings	1,000
Stock	3,000
Rent owing	50
Debtors	470
Creditors	1,200
Long-term loan from X	2,000
Van	500

Answer the following questions.

(a) What is Smith's investment (i.e. capital) in the business?
(b) What is the value of total current assets, the
(c) total current liabilities, and the
(d) value of working capital? (i.e. current assets − current liabilities).
(e) What is the capital employed or value of total assets?
(f) Is Smith solvent?

BALANCE SHEET OF SMITH CO. LTD. AS AT............

Liabilities		Assets	
....	100	....	90
....	50	....	1000
....	1200	....	3000
....	2000	....	470
....	1710	....	500
	£5060		£5060

FIG. 23.—Balance Sheet of Smith Co. Ltd.

NOTE: Check that your answers agree with the following: (a) £1,710, (b) £3,560, (c) £1,350, (d) £2,210, (e) £5,060, (f) yes, since Smith has sufficient assets to pay all debts. However, his liquidity position is less rosy because the value of debts becoming *immediately* payable exceeds the current value of money and near-money assets (*i.e.* debtors).

9. Vertical Balance Sheet. An alternative presentation of the Balance Sheet is the *vertical balance sheet*, which is preferable to the customary *side by side* form because no calculations are needed to establish working capital and net assets. G. Smith's Balance Sheet in vertical form is as follows:

BALANCE SHEET OF G. SMITH AS AT ....

Fixed assets			
Furniture and fittings			£1,000
Motor van			500
			1,500
Current assets			
Stocks		£3,000	
Debtors		470	
Cash in hand		90	
		3,560	
Less: Current liabilities			
Creditors	£1,200		
Rent owing	50		
Bank overdraft	100		
		1,350	
WORKING CAPITAL			2,210
NET ASSETS			3,710
Financed by:			
Smith's capital			1,710
Loan from X			2,000
LONGER-TERM FUNDS EMPLOYED			3,710

NOTE: For further examples of typical Balance Sheet items and relationships, *see* Fig. 25.

FIG. 24.—Vertical Balance Sheet of G. Smith Esq.

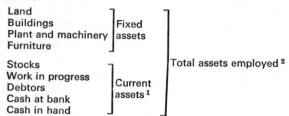

FIG. 25.—The Balance Sheet with definitions.

1–3 = current net assets or (net) working capital.
2–3 = net capital employed.
  4 = net worth.

10. Company law requirements. The *Companies Act* 1948 requires a company to keep proper books of account showing:

    (*a*) The nature and amount of all income and expenditure.
    (*b*) Its sales and purchases.
    (*c*) Its assets and liabilities.

In addition, a Profit and Loss Account or Balance Sheet must be laid before the company in general meeting at least once every calendar year; wilful non-compliance with any of the above provisions may render the directors liable to imprisonment or to a fine.

11. Contents of the Balance Sheet. The 1948 and 1967

Companies Acts demand the following information in a Balance Sheet:

(*a*) The authorised and issue share capital.

(*b*) The amount of the Share Premium Account.

(*c*) The amount of reserves.

(*d*) Details of liabilities including debentures, mortgages and long-term loans. Similarly, short-term liabilities must be disclosed including bank loans and overdrafts, trade liabilities, recommended dividends, current taxation and amounts due to subsidiaries.

(*e*) The separation of fixed and current assets.

(*f*) The method of valuation of fixed assets.

(*g*) The aggregate amounts provided for depreciation of fixed assets.

(*h*) Values of trade investments and shares in subsidiaries and any amounts due from subsidiary companies.

(*i*) Details of current assets, in particular stocks and work in progress.

(*j*) Corresponding figures at the end of the preceding financial period must be given.

(*k*) The following information must be contained within the accounts:

(*i*) Emoluments of the chairman, and

(*ii*) highest paid director, and

(*iii*) the number of directors earning up to £2,500, 2,501 to £5,000, £5,001 to £7,500 and so on, in £2,500 "bands";

(*iv*) any amounts in excess of £50 paid to a charity or political party;

(*v*) directors' names and interest in the company;

(*vi*) details of subsidiaries.

WORKING CAPITAL

12. Nature of working capital. Working capital is the difference between current assets and current liabilities and represents the amount of money the company must find to augment creditors' funds in order to finance its day-to-day trade. At any one point in time money will be locked up in current assets, *i.e.* stocks of raw materials, work in progress, finished goods and debtors, the total value of which determines the amount of money that must be found.

EXAMPLE (*a*)

Total current assets	£10,000
Less: Current liabilities	8,000
Working capital	£2,000

In example (*a*), creditors finance £8,000 of the £10,000 worth of current assets, and the company itself finances the balance of £2,000.

EXAMPLE (*b*)

Total fixed assets		£20,000
Total current assets	£10,000	
Less: Current liabilities	11,000	
Deficiency in working capital	1,000	
		1,000
Net assets		£19,000

In example (*b*), outsiders have contributed £11,000 which finances current assets completely so that the balance of £1,000 spills over into fixed assets. Clearly in this case the company has a negative working capital; all current assets and £1,000 worth of fixed assets are financed by creditors.

13. Determinants of working capital. The amount of working capital required by a business is determined by the following:

(*a*) The value of expenditure on wages, raw materials and direct overheads incurred in the production of saleable goods.

(*b*) The length of the production/sales cycle, *i.e.* from when costs are incurred on production to when sales are paid for.

(*c*) The value of expenditure on indirect overheads during this period.

(*d*) The amount of credit received from creditors and the length of the credit.

14. Calculation of working capital. The value of working capital required to finance its day-to-day trade may be calculated by quantifying the determinants above. Imagine that:

(*a*) Anticipated sales revenue is £100,000.

(b) Raw materials cost 40p per £1 of sales and are held in stock prior to production for one week.

(c) Direct wages and expenses are 50p per £1 of sales.

(d) The production cycle is two weeks.

(e) Stocks of finished goods are held for an average period of two weeks before they are sold.

(f) Creditors supply materials on credit for six weeks.

(g) All sales are credit sales and four weeks credit is granted.

  (i) *Raw materials held in stock*
      financing period × cost/£1 sales × sales revenue
      1/52 × £0·40 × £100,000   =   £769

  (ii) *Materials used in production*
      2/52 × £0·40 × £100,000   =   1,538

  (iii) *Labour and expenses**
      2/52 × £0·50 × £100,000 ÷ 2 =   961

  (iv) *Stocks of finished goods*
      2/52 × £0·90 × £100,000   =   3,461

  (v) *Debtors*
      4/52 × £100,000   =   7,692

CASH NEEDED TO FINANCE CURRENT
ASSETS   14,421
deduct cash provided by creditors
  (vi) *Creditors*
      6/52 × £0·40 × £100,000   =   4,615

TOTAL WORKING CAPITAL REQUIRED TO FINANCE
DAY-TO-DAY TRADE   = £9,806

*Labour and direct expenses are not incurred at the beginning of the cycle but evenly over the period and are therefore divided by 2 to establish the average value of such costs over the two-week period.

FUNDS FLOW STATEMENT

15. Funds flow statement. Each year an increasing number of public companies are including in their published accounts a funds flow statement. Indeed it is one of the most useful methods that gives shareholders an idea of where company funds have come from and how they are employed. If sufficiently detailed, it will highlight company progress and problems.

Basically, one is comparing the Balance Sheets of a company at two different dates and noting the changes that have occurred over the period.* For example, if an examination reveals that the value of an asset has fallen, then less money is now tied up so it must represent a source of funds. Similarly, if a liability has increased then money or money's worth has been received by the company and again it is a source of funds. Conversely an increase in an asset or decrease in a liability represents a use of funds.

This is summarised below:

Source of funds:

    (a) Decrease in an asset.

    (b) Increase in a liability.

Use of funds:

    (a) Increase in an asset.

    (b) Decrease in a liability.

16. Example. Suppose a company publishes two Balance Sheets for the dates 31.12.75 and 31.12.76, then we may compare the items and draw up a simple Funds Flow Statement.

FUNDS FLOW STATEMENT FOR THE YEAR ENDED 31.12.76

Assets:	31.12.75	31.12.76	Source	Use
	£K	£K	£K	£K
Net fixed assets	125	165		40
Stocks	25	30		5
Debtors	15	20		5
Cash	20	5	15	
	—	—		
Total assets	185	220		
	═	═		
Financed by:				
Share capital	60	90	30	
Undistributed profit	30	40	10	
Secured bank loan	60	60		
Creditors	35	30		5
	—	—	—	—
	185	220	55	55
	═	═	═	═

FIG. 26.—A Funds Flow Statement.

*Only those items that effect changes in *cash* are included in a Source and Use of Funds statement.

This statement tells us that there has been a significant increase in fixed assets (£40K) with modest increases in stocks and debtors and a decrease in trade creditors. How has this been financed? It appears sensible that the sizeable long-term investment in fixed assets has been paid for by long-term sources of funds, namely extra share capital for share holders (£30K) and undistributed profits (£10K), *i.e.* the long-term use is matched by a long-term source. As far as short-term items are concerned, cash has been used to finance the higher stocks and debtors and also to pay off some of the creditors.

EXAMPLE. Examine the following Balance Sheets and complete the *Sources* and *Uses* columns and note the main changes in the company's financial position.

Assets:	31.12.75	31.12.76	Source	Use
	£K	£K	£	£K
Gross fixed assets	100	120		20
Less: Depreciation	40	50	10	
Net fixed assets	60	70	—	— (10)
Stocks	20	30		(3)
Debtors	15	18		
Cash	10	2	(8)	
Total assets	105	120		

Financed by:				
Share capital	50	65	15	
Undistributed profit	30	35	5	
Debentures	—	10	10	
Secured bank loan	9	—		(9)
Creditors	16	10		(6)
Total	105	120	48	48

17. Changes in working capital. Working capital is the difference between current assets and current liabilities. An alternative way of presenting a Funds Flow Statement so that the change in working capital is highlighted is as follows:

	£K		£K
Retained profit	5	Increase in fixed assets	20
Add depreciation	10	Repayment of bank loan	9
Total trading sources	15	Change in working capital (increase)	11
Proceeds from shareholders	15		
Proceeds from debentures	10		
Total non-trading sources	25		
TOTAL SOURCES	40	TOTAL USES	40

STATEMENT OF CHANGE IN WORKING CAPITAL

Sources	£K	Uses	£K
Cash	8	Stocks	10
		Debtors	3
Net use of working capital (increase)	11	Creditors	6
TOTAL	19	TOTAL	19

FIG. 27.—Statement of change in working capital.

The above statement reveals that trading sources of funds is insufficient to finance the extra fixed assets and repay the bank loan. Consequently, extra shares have been issued and debentures raised and the surplus of £11K used to finance extra working capital. The accompanying statement of the change in working capital reveals how the individual items of current assets and current liabilities have changed and account for the balance of £11K; the amount by which total uses exceed total sources. Thus in the areas outside working capital, sources have exceeded uses by £11K. In the working capital area extra cash of £8K is released and the total £19K used to finance stocks, debtors and pay off creditors.

EXAMPLE. **Movement of funds problem.** Examine the Balance Sheets of Dog Company Limited and complete the accompanying Movement of Funds Statement to confirm that working capital decreases by £17,500.

BALANCE SHEET OF DOG CO. LTD. AS AT 31.12.76

	Year 1	2		Year 1	2
Capital			**Fixed assets**		
60,000 £1 ordinary shares	£60,000	£60,000	Land and buildings	£50,000	£60,000
Revenue reserve	13,500	23,500	Plant and machinery	7,500	10,000
	£73,500	£83,500		£57,500	£70,000
			Current Assets		
			Trade investments	25,000	15,000
Debentures	40,000	30,000	Raw materials	12,000	14,000
Loan from parent company	5,000	—	Stocks	20,000	15,000
Current Liabilities			Debtors	5,000	2,000
Trade creditors	2,000	3,000	Cash	7,000	5,000
Short-term bank loan	5,000	3,000			
Tax payable	1,000	1,500			
	£126,500	£121,000		£126,500	£121,000

Fig. 28.—Balance Sheet of Dog Co. Ltd.

During Year 2 the company bought plant and machinery for £3,000 and made a provision of £500 for depreciation. Profits retained are £10,000.

MOVEMENT OF FUNDS STATEMENT

Net profit retained	10000	Expenditure on assets £ 13000	
+ depreciation	500	Repayments of long-term loans	
TOTAL TRADING SOURCE £ 10,500			10000
			5000
Extra shares issued	NIL		
Extra debentures	NIL		
		Increase (decrease) in Working capital	(17,500)
TOTAL EXTERNAL SOURCES £			
TOTAL SOURCES £ 10,500		TOTAL USES £ 10,500	

Fig. 29.—Movement of Funds Statement.

CHANGE IN WORKING CAPITAL

Increase in creditors	1000	or	Decrease in creditors		
Increase in taxation		or	Decrease in taxation		
Decrease in stocks	5000	or	Increase in stocks	~~3000~~	
Decrease in trade investm't	10000	or	Increase in trade investm't		
Decrease in debtors	3000	or	Increase in debtors		
Increase in bank loan		or	Decrease in bank loan	2000	
Decrease in cash	2000	or	Increase in cash		
Net increase in Working capital		or	Net decrease in Working capital	17500	
TOTAL	£ 19500		TOTAL	£ 19500	

Fig. 30.—Change in working capital.

EXAMPLE. **Construction of Balance Sheets.** Test your understanding of the structure of the Balance Sheet and the relationship between assets and liabilities by drawing up separate Balance Sheets after each of the following transactions.

1.1.76	Y forms a company, Y Limited, issuing 25,000 £1 ordinary shares for cash.
2.1.76	Y Limited buys premises for £10,000 cash.
3.1.76	Y Limited buys £5,000 worth of goods on credit.
4.1.76	Y Limited spends £2,000 cash to convert stocks valued at £1,000 cost into finished goods.
5.1.76	Sells all finished stocks for £6,000: half on credit and half for cash.
6.1.76	Revalues premises to £15,000.
7.1.76	Borrows £10,000 from his bank.

Answer:

BALANCE SHEET OF Y CO. LTD. AS AT 1.1.76

Capital:		*Current assets*:	
25,000 shares @ £1	£25,000	Cash	£25,000
	£25,000		£25,000

BALANCE SHEET OF Y CO. LTD. AS AT 2.1.76

Capital:		*Fixed assets*:	
25,000 shares @ £1	£25,000	Land and buildings	£10,000
		Current assets:	
		Cash	£15,000
	£25,000		£25,000

Fig. 31.—Balance Sheets of Y Co. Ltd.

Summary of Balance Sheet items :

3.1.76   Share capital £25,000, creditors £5,000, land and buildings £10,000, cash £15,000, stocks of raw materials £5,000.

4.1.76   Share capital £25,000, creditors £5,000, land and buildings £10,000, cash £13,000, stocks of raw materials £4,000, stocks of finished goods £3,000.

5.1.76   Share capital £25,000, profit retained £3,000, creditors £5,000, land and buildings £10,000, cash £16,000, stocks of raw materials £4,000, debtors £3,000.

6.1.76   Share capital £25,000, retained profit £3,000, capital reserve £5,000, creditors £5,000, land and buildings £15,000, cash £16,000, stocks of materials £4,000, debtors £3,000.

7.1.76   Share capital £25,000, retained profit £3,000, capital reserve £5,000, creditors £5,000, bank loan £10,000, land and buildings £15,000, cash £26,000, stocks of materials £4,000, debtors £3,000.

PROGRESS TEST 6

1. Explain the following:
"Owners funds = assets less creditors." **(1–3)**
2. What does a balance sheet contain? **(9–11)**

PART TWO

MONEY: HOW WELL DO WE USE IT?

We are now in a position to build on the foundations of Part One where we considered the questions of where money came from and how we recorded it. Clearly the purpose of business is not to obtain and hold money but instead to use it in an attempt to attain the objectives set by management or the shareholders. Therefore we now turn our attention to the way management uses money by examining first the Profit and Loss Account and then general company performance, measured in historical terms by analysis of company accounts, and also under conditions of inflation.

CHAPTER VII

PROFIT AND LOSS

THE TRADING, PROFIT AND LOSS ACCOUNT

1. Purpose of the Trading, Profit and Loss Account. Preparing a Trading, Profit and Loss Account is rather like taking a ciné film of a company's transactions. It summarises transactions over the complete trading period to show how successful the company has been in making profits. At the end of the trading period the very last frame is extracted and blown up to show the financial position at that moment in time. This record is the Balance Sheet.

The purpose of a Trading and Profit and Loss Account is twofold:

(a) It measures the size of the profit or loss for the trading period.

(b) It indicates the factors that have caused profits to rise or fall.

The actual period covered by the account is determined by the management and in practice may be compiled monthly, quarterly or half-yearly for management information purposes, although for taxation and reporting reasons, it is drawn up at least once every calendar year. Thus it is usually headed as *Profit and Loss Account of X Co. Ltd. for the year ended 31st December 19—* (or the appropriate date).

It summarises all sales revenue, both cash and credit and any other source of trading income over the period, all cash and credit purchases of goods for conversion or resale and all other trading expenses and overheads that become due or are incurred over the period (*see* IV and V).

2. Structure of the Trading and Profit and Loss Account. It is common practice to divide the account into two parts:

(*a*) The *Trading Account* calculates the gross profit or mark up which shows how much must be earned gross to cover the business expenses and leave an acceptable profit. This is expressed as:

GROSS PROFIT = SALES REVENUE — COST OF SALES

(*b*) The *Profit and Loss Account* charges selling, establishment and financial expenses against the gross profit to arrive at net profits that may be apportioned to the owners of the business. Thus:

NET PROFIT = GROSS PROFIT — INDIRECT EXPENSES

3. Margin and mark-up. There is widespread confusion over the meaning of these terms; often they are used in the wrong context and reveal ignorance of their true meaning.

Margin should always be related to sales price, and mark-up to cost, *i.e.* if a person buys something for £1 and adds a mark-up of 50 per cent, then selling price is £1·50. To get back to cost we must subtract the margin of $33\frac{1}{3}$ per cent (*i.e.* 50 per cent on costs is equivalent to 33·3 per cent off sales).

(*a*) To calculate the margin:

$$\frac{\text{Mark-up} \times 100}{100 + \text{Mark up}}$$

(*b*) To calculate the mark up:

$$\frac{\text{Margin} \times 100}{100 - \text{Margin}}$$

4. Exercise. Margin and mark-up:

(*a*) Calculate the margin if the mark-up on costs is 37 per cent.

(*b*) Calculate the mark-up if the margin on sales is 42 per cent.

5. Capital and revenue expenditure. In order to understand fully the nature of the Profit and Loss Account and the meaning of profit, it is important to appreciate the difference between capital and revenue expenditure. The following example illustrates the essential differences.

(*a*) *Capital expenditure.* Long-term expenditure on something that is used in the generation of output and profit is called *capital.* It means that one asset (cash) is exchanged for another asset. It is recorded under *fixed assets* in the Balance Sheet.

(*b*) *Revenue expenditure.* Expenditure incurred in the production of sales and in the day-to-day running of the business is called *revenue.* It is recorded in the Profit and Loss Account.

6. Problem: Examine the following expenditures and allocate them between capital and revenue.

Expenditure: capital *or* revenue?

1. Wages
2. Raw materials used in production
3. Land
4. Rent
5. Hydraulic press
6. Motor van
7. Motor van running expenses
8. Insurance on building
9. Heat and light
10. Depreciation on van
11. Rates
12. Advertising
13. Office furniture
14. Office wages

NOTE: Revenue expenditure: 1, 2, 4, 7, 8, 9, 10, 11, 12, 14
Capital expenditure: 3, 5, 6, 13.

7. Trading and Profit and Loss. Let us imagine a retailer who buys goods for resale for a cost of £60,000, and whose customary mark-up is 50 per cent. With this information we can write up his Trading Account and calculate his gross profit (a — b = c in the Trading and Profit and Loss Account on p. 104). Furthermore he incurs several expenses over the trading period which he lists (*see* below).

	£	1 *Selling and distri- bution* £	2 *Admin- istration* £	3 *Finance* £
Advertising	1,000	1,000	—	—
General office salaries	6,000			
Interest on bank loan	200			
Salesmen's wages	7,000			
Rent on premises	900			
Rates on premises	300			
Bank charges	60			
Lighting and heating for premises	300			
Delivery van expenses	800			
Depreciation on delivery vans	200			
Accountants salaries	5,000			
Total expenses	£21,760	£9,750	£6,500	£5,510

He wishes to charge these expenses against the appropriate department and although certain expenditures are clearly identified by department, *e.g.* advertising to Selling Department, others are incurred for the benefit of several departments. Assuming that he decides to apportion these expenses on the basis of the area of each department (Selling Department 30,000 sq. ft., Administration 20,000 sq. ft. and Finance Department 10,000 sq. ft.) complete columns 1, 2 and 3 in the above list, ensuring that the sum of each agrees with the totals.

We can now complete his Profit and Loss Account by charging the totals for Selling (d), Administration (e), and Finance (f) against the gross profit. The effect is that the retailer earns a *net profit* of £8,240, *i.e.* c — (d + e + f).

TRADING AND PROFIT AND LOSS ACCOUNT FOR A RETAILER FOR THE PERIOD ENDED ....

Sales (a) *i.e.* £60,000 + 50%		£90,000
Less: Cost of sales (b)		60,000
Gross profit (c)		30,000
Less: Selling and distribution expenses		
(d)	£9,750	
Administration expenses (e)	6,500	
Financial expenses (f)	5,510	21,760
Net profit		£8,240

8. Profit and Loss Account. Figure 32 illustrates a typical Profit and Loss Account of a branch of a department store. In this case the Trading Account is superfluous, for the gross profit figure can be calculated by reference to the percentage margin on sales (*see* the previous example where a 50 per cent mark-up produces a 33·3 per cent gross margin on sales; thus if sales are £90,000 the gross profit is 33·3 per cent or £30,000).

The branch manager can see at a glance how the figures compare with corresponding figures for the previous year, and which category of costs are increasing in relation to sales turnover. Costs to sales figures that have increased are clearly identified and these areas can be examined for possible cost savings.

For example, current year sales and gross profits are higher than the previous year and this is reflected by the total net revenues as percentages of sales (32 and 31 per cent respectively). Investigation may show this to be the result of more efficient buying or higher selling prices or a combination of both. However, this advantage is not maintained, for although total administration costs to sales (8 per cent), total occupancy costs to sales (10 per cent), total despatch costs to sales (2 per cent), and head office costs to sales (2 per cent) are in line with last year, total selling costs to sales have increased from 5 to 6 per cent and have eliminated the profit advantage so that current net profit to sales is identical to last year at 4 per cent.

An efficient manager would now ask the question "Why?" and discover whether the cause is controllable. The answer could be that salesmens' wages have increased, which is

SUPERSTORES GROUP LTD.

Branch Profit and Loss Account

| | THIS YEAR | | LAST YEAR | |
	Amount £000	% on sales (£500,000)	Amount £000	% on sales (£400,000)
NET REVENUE				
Gross profit on sales	150	30	116	29
Service charge on H.P. contracts	10	2	8	2
TOTAL NET REVENUE	160	32	124	31
Less: EXPENDITURE				
1. ADMINISTRATIVE				
Office staff salaries				
State graduated pension scheme				
Company pension scheme				
National Insurance				
Office equipment maintenance				
Travelling expenses				
Postage				
Telephone				
Miscellaneous				
TOTAL ADMINISTRATIVE	40	8	32	8
2. OCCUPANCY				
Rent				
Rates				
Light, heat, power and water				
Premises maintenance repairs and cleaning				
Depreciation of fixtures and fittings				
Miscellaneous				
TOTAL OCCUPANCY	50	10	40	10
3. SELLING				
Salaries, wages and commissions:				
Managers and assistants				
Showroom assistants				
Travelling expenses				
Depreciation of motor vehicles				
Miscellaneous				
TOTAL SELLING	30	6	20	5
4. DESPATCH				
Parcel post and carriage				
Motor vehicle expenses				
Depreciation of motor vehicles				
Miscellaneous				
TOTAL DESPATCH	10	2	8	2
5. HEAD OFFICE EXPENSES*	10	2	8	2
TOTAL EXPENDITURE	140	28	108	27
BRANCH NET PROFIT	20	4	16	4

*Head Office is administrative and earns no revenue: its costs are apportioned among the revenue earning branches in proportion to their sales revenue.

Fig. 32.—Profit and Loss Account of Superstores Group Ltd.

self-explanatory, or it could be that travelling expenses are significantly higher, in which case the increases need to be examined.

However, one word of warning: the branch manager should interpret these figures with caution, for although such comparisons are admirable in that they establish targets for future years and through analysis of the variances provide control, the component figures may become distorted by exceptional circumstances that management is unaware of, and therefore form unrealistic standards in normal trading activities. For example, the total selling costs last year might have been low because of a shortage of salesmen which has been remedied in the current year. The increased sales revenue may very well be due to the contributions of these new salesmen and instead, attention should be given to other areas for cost savings, particularly administration and occupancy. Intuitively one would expect some economies of scale in these areas, *i.e.* they consist largely of fixed costs and so should not increase in proportion to sales.

9. Manufacturing Accounts. It is usual for a company whose operations include the manufacture of goods to divide the Trading Account into two parts:

(a) *The Manufacturing Account* that measures the cost of production of the goods produced during the period.

(b) *The Trading Account* that calculates the gross profit.

The Manufacturing Account should show the *prime costs*, *i.e.* the total costs of materials, wages and identifiable expenses of production, and the *factory costs* which consist of prime costs plus indirect expenses. The latter costs are those expenses that are incurred in the production process but which cannot be identified with specific outputs. Occasionally the goods are transferred to the Trading Account at above cost, in which case the Manufacturing Account makes a profit which should be transferred into the Profit and Loss Account. If the transfer is made at market price then it represents the profit (or loss) of making the goods instead of buying them ready made, *i.e.* the relative efficiency of the factory.

The Manufacturing, Trading and Profit and Loss Account below illustrates the layout of typical cost and revenue items.

MANUFACTURING, TRADING AND PROFIT AND PROFIT AND LOSS ACCOUNT OF PORCUPINE CO. LTD. FOR THE YEAR ENDED 31.12.76

Manufacturing Account

	£	£		£
Materials consumed			Factory cost of finished	
Opening stock	10,000		goods (transferred to	
Purchases (*Less*: Returns)	40,000		Trading Account)	68,000
	50,000			
Less: Closing stock	15,000			
		35,000		
Manufacturing wages		25,000		
PRIME COST		60,000		
Factory expenses				
Light, heat, power	3,000			
Rent and rates	1,000			
Maintenance	3,000			
Depreciation of plant	2,000			
		9,000		
		69,000		
Work in progress				
At commencement of period	3,000			
Less: At end of period	4,000	(1,000)		
FACTORY COST OF FINISHED				
GOODS		£68,000		£68,000

Trading Account

	£	£		£
Opening stock of finished			Sales	120,000
goods	7,000			
Production costs (from				
Manufacturing Account)	68,000			
	75,000			
Less: Closing stock of finished				
goods	6,000			
COST OF SALES	69,000			
GROSS PROFIT (transferred				
to Profit and Loss Account)	51,000			
	£120,000			£120,000

Profit and Loss Account

	£	£		£
Administration expenses		14,000	Gross profit (from	
Selling expenses		6,000	Trading Account)	51,000
Distribution expenses				
Transport outwards	4,000			
Depreciation on vans	1,000			
		5,000		
Financial expenses		5,000		
Bad debts provision	1,000			
Debenture interest	2,000	3,000		
NET PROFIT BEFORE TAX		18,000		
		£51,000		£51,000

Fig. 33.—Manufacturing, Trading and Profit and Loss Account of Porcupine Co. Ltd.

10. Meaning of profits and losses.

(a) *Gross profit* is the excess of the selling price over the direct costs of purchase or production of a good or goods.

(b) *Gross loss* is the excess of the direct costs of purchase or production over the selling price of a good or goods.

(c) *Net profit* is that amount by which the excess of the selling price of a good or goods over the direct costs of purchase or production which together with any other income exceeds the overhead costs of the organisation.

(d) *Net loss* is that amount by which overheads and direct costs of purchase or production exceed the selling price of a good or goods together with any other income.

11. Ways to increase profits. In general terms, profit means the difference between sales revenue and the costs of bringing the goods into a saleable state. It is usual accounting practice to show in the company's Trading Account the gross profit as a percentage of sales revenue so that one can tell at a glance whether trading profits on sales have improved in comparison with previous periods. For instance:

	1972		1973		1974	
	£	%	£	%	£	%
Sales	10,000	100	10,000	100	12,000	100
Less: Cost of sales	8,000	80	7,500	75	9,000	75
Gross profit	2,000	20	2,500	25	3,000	25

Compared with 1972, management traded more efficiently in 1973 and 1974 and so improved the gross profit margin from 20 to 25 per cent. Furthermore, since sales revenue is unchanged between 1972 and 1973 the gross profit value is increased. This is only one way of improving profits. In summary, profits can be increased by the following measures:

(a) Increasing prices and sales revenue, *ceteris paribus* (all other things remaining equal).

(b) Reducing cost of sales, *ceteris paribus*.

(c) Understating the value or quality of opening stock in trade.

(d) Overstating the value or quality of closing stock in trade.

Points (*a*) and (*b*) are self-evident but (*c*) and (*d*) require further examination.

12. How stock valuation affects profit. Consider an example. The actual stock in trade position is shown below (column *i*). However, by varying the value of opening and closing stocks (columns *ii* and *iii*) we can affect profits.

	i		*ii*		*iii*	
Sales		£10,000		£10,000		£10,000
Opening stock	£1,000		£ 800		£1,000	
Add: Purchases	4,000		4,000		4,000	
	5,000		4,800		5,000	
Less: Closing stock	2,000		2,000		2,500	
Less: Cost of sales		3,000		2,800		2,500
Gross profit		7,000		7,200		7,500

Column *ii* shows that if opening stock is understated then cost of sales is reduced and profit "increased" by a corresponding amount.

In column *iii* an inflated closing stock figure produces a similar increase in profit.

Obviously the positions shown in columns *ii* and *iii* cannot in any sense represent a "true and fair" view of the company's profits, and to meet this company law requirement, clearly defined principles must be applied consistently in all stock valuations.

13. Valuation of stocks in trade. Stocks may be valued as follows :

(*a*) *Cost* which is made up of prime costs and may include additional direct expenses involved in bringing the goods to their present location or condition, and a proportion of overheads, excepting selling and distribution expenses.

(*b*) *Cost* or *market value* whichever is the lower.

(*c*) *Cost, market value,* or *replacement value,* whichever is the lower.

PROGRESS TEST 7

1. Why are Trading and Profit and Loss Accounts prepared? (1–8)

2. Explain precisely the relationships between the Manufacturing, the Trading and the Profit and Loss Accounts. (9–10)

CHAPTER VIII

MEASURING COMPANY PERFORMANCE

INTERPRETATION OF COMPANY ACCOUNTS

1. Meaning of company accounts. Company accounts refer to the Trading and Profit and Loss Account and the Balance Sheet. The former provides an historic assessment of the company's trading position, *i.e.* a "true and fair view" of the profit or loss for the financial year; the latter gives "a true and fair view" of the company's financial position at the time of the statement.

The qualities (true and fair) demanded of accounts by the *Companies Acts* are unfortunately undefined but are interpreted to mean "reality and objectivity." In other words, there is a duty on the part of the accountant preparing these accounts to interpret all company transactions as objectively as possible and thereby conforming to the accepted standards on accountancy conventions in that industry or trade. On the other hand, "reality" calls for the reporting of transactions that are genuinely different or unusual.

Details set out in these accounts laid before the company in general meeting and thereafter possibly published in the financial press and lodged in Companies House are carefully analysed by interested parties for a variety of reasons.

2. Persons interested in company accounts.

(*a*) *Management.* Managers wish to compare their performance with selected market and profitability objectives and with performance of competitors.

(*b*) *Ordinary shareholders.*

(*i*) Short-term income maximisers look for distribution of earnings, *i.e.* the amount of dividend declared.

(*ii*) Those who take a longer-term view are more interested in profit retention for future growth in earnings and capital appreciation.

(*iii*) Prospective shareholders examine the company's

profitability earning potential and risk *vis-à-vis* alternative investments.

(c) *Preference shareholders.* These look for stable profits at a level that provides adequate dividend cover.

(d) *Debenture holders.* These as individuals, banks or finance companies keep a close watch on the level of current and future earnings and the valuation of assets that cover the debt.

(e) *Creditors and bankers.* They ascertain the value of prior charges since they rely on sufficiency of uncharged assets to provide security for their claims.

(f) *Offerors.* These are interested in the company's earning potential and the possibility of acquiring assets at a discount, *i.e.* buying the shares at below their real value.

(g) *Financial analysts, investment advisers* and *speculators* on the Stock Exchange. They compare the Balance Sheet valuation of the company's shares with the Stock Exchange valuation and the yield in relation to opportunity cost (*i.e.* the yield in comparison with the yield of alternative investments).

(h) *Trades Unions.* Unions compare directors' and shareholders' earnings with union members' wages.

3. Criteria for examination. In summary, these observers are motivated to analyse the published accounts on one or more of the following grounds:

(a) Profitability.
(b) Activity.
(c) Solvency.
(d) Gearing and capital structure.
(e) Ownership and control.

4. Sources of information. The Balance Sheet, with notes to the Balance Sheet and the Profit and Loss Account, are the main sources of information because companies are under a statutory duty to publish annually, and include details specified in the *Companies Acts, e.g.* sales revenue, profit, the company's valuation of its investments, value of fixed and current assets, depreciation provided, authorised and issued share capital, payments to directors, the total of long-term loans made to the company and the interest payable, etc.

Additional information that enables observers to assess

company performance in terms of the above criteria is found in the following:

(a) *The Directors' Report.* This is attached to the Balance Sheet and contains details of the dividend the directors are recommending with a report on the company's state of affairs for the benefit of the shareholders. Naturally, trade secrets or details that could be damaging are not reported.

(b) *The Register of Charges.* This register is kept at the company's registered office and contains details of all charges on the company's property. It is freely available for inspection by shareholders and creditors and to others for a modest fee.

(c) *The Register of Shareholders' Interests.* This records the names and addresses of shareholders of the company and their number of shares. In addition it contains an index of shareholders' names who have an interest in 10 per cent or more of the shares of any class of capital which carry voting rights. The register is freely available for inspection and in conjunction with the *Register of Directors' Interests* provides a clue to the true owners of the company.

(d) *Memorandum and Articles of Association.* The former states the constitution of the company and defines its powers and objects, while the latter contains the rules on how company affairs are to be conducted, the rights of members, and the duties and powers of directors.

CRITERIA FOR EXAMINATION OF COMPANY ACCOUNTS

5. Introduction. In this section we consider the five selected criteria for examination of company accounts listed in **3**, namely profitability, activity, solvency, gearing and capital structure and finally ownership and control in relation to the sources of information outlined in **4**. The whole relationship can be visualised in the matrix found in Table VII.

The Balance Sheet and the summarised Profit and Loss Account of the Lemming Co. Ltd. are used to illustrate how company accounts may be interpreted using our selected criteria (*see* Figs. 34 and 35).

The following ratios and financial analysis may appear rather formidable especially for the manager who has minimal

BALANCE SHEET OF THE LEMMING CO. LTD. AS AT 31.3.76

	31.3.75 £	31.3.76 £		1975	1976	31.3.75 £	31.3.76 £
Share Capital and Reserves			**Fixed Assets**				
Authorised Share Capital			Land and buildings			60,000	60,000
150,000 £1 ordinary shares			Plant and machinery				
10,000 10% £1 Preference Shares			Cost	40,000	40,000		
			Less Depreciation	15,000	20,000		
				25,000	20,000	25,000	20,000
Issued Share Capital			**Total Fixed Assets**			85,000	80,000
100,000 £1 ordinary shares	100,000	100,000					
10,000 £1 preference shares	10,000	10,000	**Current Assets**				
Revenue Reserves	20,000	25,000	Stocks			40,000	46,000
			Debtors			52,000	65,000
10% Debentures	10,000	10,000	Cash			5,000	—
Deferred liability							
Corporation tax due 1.1.76	2,000						
1.1.77		3,000					
Current Liabilities							
Creditors	30,000	28,000					
Dividend payable	10,000	10,000					
Bank Overdraft	—	5,000					
	182,000	191,000				182,000	191,000

Signed:................

FIG. 34.—Balance Sheet of Lemming Co. Ltd.

Contingent liability: the contractors who built the plant have brought an action against the Lemming Co. Ltd. which together with a claim by the architects could involve liability amounting to £25,000. The directors propose a dividend to the ordinary shareholders of 10 per cent.

EXTRACTS FROM TRADING AND PROFIT AND LOSS ACCOUNT FOR YEAR ENDED 31.1.76
(PREVIOUS YEAR'S FIGURES IN BRACKETS)

Gross Sales	245,000	(230,000)
Less Cost of Sales	200,000	(190,000)
Gross Profit	45,000	(40,000)
Debenture interest	1,000	(1,000)
Net Profit before Tax	31,000	(28,000)
Net Profit after Tax	16,000	(15,000)
Dividends Preference	1,000	(1,000)
Ordinary	10,000	(10,000)
Net Profit retained	5,000	(4,000)

FIG. 35.—Summarised Trading and Profit and Loss Account of the Lemming Co. Ltd. (Selected figures to illustrate the use of ratios.)

TABLE VII.—SELECTED CRITERIA FOR EXAMINATION OF COMPANY ACCOUNTS.

Source of information	Profitability	Activity	Solvency	Gearing and capital structure	Ownership and control
Register of charges			1. Value of assets not charged		1. Percentage of company assets charged and nature of charges
Register of shareholders' interests					1. Shareholders with 10% or more of class of voting share capital
Memorandum and articles of association			1. Company borrowing powers	1. Debenture and Preference shares redemption date	1. Voting rights of classes of capital
Trading and profit and loss account	1. Gross profit 2. Net profit after tax	1. Sales Revenue			
Balance sheet	1. Change in Revenue Reserve 2. Final dividends declared	1. Movements in assets	1. Capital uncalled 2. Value of net current assets 3. Estimate of contingent liabilities	1. Equity capital 2. Preference and "loan" capital and annual charges	1. Authorised and issued share capital and classes of share capital
Ratio analysis	1. $R.O.C.E. = \dfrac{N.P.\ before\ tax\ \&\ Int.}{Total\ Assets}$ 2. $R.O.I. = \dfrac{Net\ Profit\ after\ tax}{Share\ capital + Res.}$ 3. Margins on Sales $Gross = \dfrac{Gross\ Profit}{Sales}$ $Net = \dfrac{Net\ Profit}{Sales}$	1. $\dfrac{Sales}{Stocks}$ 2. $\dfrac{Debtors}{Sales}$ 3. $\dfrac{Current\ Assets}{Sales}$ 4. $\dfrac{Fixed\ Assets}{Sales}$ 5. $\dfrac{Sales}{Total\ Assets}$	1. $Current\ Ratio = \dfrac{Current\ Assets}{Current\ Liabilities}$ 2. $Quick\ Ratio = \dfrac{Liquid\ Assets}{Current\ Liabilities}$ 3. $Average\ Collection\ period = \dfrac{Debtors}{Average\ Daily\ Sales}$	1. $Debt\ Ratio = \dfrac{Net\ Worth}{Total\ Debt}$ 2. $Times\ Interest\ Earned = \dfrac{Profit\ before\ Tax\ \&\ Int.}{Interest\ Charges}$ 3. $\dfrac{Net\ Worth}{Fixed\ Assets}$ 4. $Gearing\ factor = \dfrac{Fixed\ "interest"\ cap'l.}{Ordinary\ Shares}$	1. $Vote\ gearing = \dfrac{Total\ Capital}{Total\ Voting\ Capital}$

financial knowledge; nevertheless, he should persevere and work through the examples encouraged by the knowledge that they represent a well-tried tool in financial planning and control. Clearly a quantitative approach removes a good deal of the guessing on the part of management; clear financial targets are established and performance closely controlled for the optimum use of the resources of the business. Arnold Weinstock, chief executive of G.E.C., has built up an outstanding reputation as an exponent of ratio analysis and through this "style of management" has transformed unprofitable companies into efficient giants in the electrical industry; clear evidence of the practical value of financial analysis.

PROFITABILITY

6. Gross and net profit. In order to assess the performance of the Lemming Co. Ltd. in terms of profitability we note from the matrix in Table VII that the first source of information on this subject is the Trading and Profit and Loss Account. This account indicates the 1976 gross profit and net profit post-tax figures to be £45,000 and £16,000 respectively. However, these figures mean little by themselves; if we compare them with the respective figures for the previous year (£40,000 and £15,000) they become more meaningful. In fact we see that in the year to 31.3.76, Lemming Co. Ltd. has been more profitable than in the preceding year. However, this may be due to one of several reasons unconnected with the efficiency of the company. For example, general inflation, or sales of old stocks made from low cost materials may be the reason. In order to assess and interpret company performance more accurately and on a comparable basis we rely on a ratio; expressing one figure in terms of another. The matrix indicates the main ones we will use.

(a) *Change in revenue reserve.* The Balance Sheet shows that the company has retained an additional £5,000 after payment of dividends.

(b) *The dividend.* The Balance Sheet note states that the directors propose a dividend of 10 per cent, or 10p per share. By itself this figure is not very meaningful; an investor receiving the 10p share will calculate its yield or return in relation to this investment and compare this with alternative investments.

Assume that the current share price is £2·00.

$$\text{Dividend yield} = \frac{\text{dividend paid}}{\text{share price}} \times 100$$
$$= \frac{10\text{p}}{200\text{p}} \times 100$$
$$= 5\%$$

If the average yield for this industry is 7 per cent, then present and prospective investors will naturally become disenchanted with the current dividend policy of Lemming Co. Ltd. and in consequence the share price of £2 will be marked down.

To say that a company makes £10,000 profit in 1976 does not really tell us very much about the performance of the company. It may employ £100,000 capital or £1,000,000 capital to generate this profit. Therefore to assess performance in terms of profitability we must relate profits to capital employed.

7. Return on capital employed.

$$\text{R.O.C.E.} = \frac{\text{Net profit before tax and interest}}{\text{Gross capital employed (total assets)}} \times 100$$

The Profit and Loss Account for the year ended 31.3.76 shows the pre-tax profit figure to be £31,000. However, this is after charging interest on the debenture and so £1,000 must be added back, making the numerator in the above fraction £32,000. The reasons for using the profit figure before tax and interest are as follows:

(a) Company tax liability varies according to *Finance Act* requirements. Unfortunately, *Finance Acts* are beyond the control of managers and consequently it is useful to use the profit figure that does reflect the performance of management, *i.e.* pre-tax profit. Nevertheless there is a case for taking the post-tax figure on the grounds that tax minimisation is a responsibility of management and the post-tax figure reflects their performance in this area.

(b) Interest is added back to the profit figure because we

want to measure the total return (*i.e.* profit plus interest payments) resulting from the employment of the total sources of finance, whether it be share or loan capital.

If we apply the above formulae, then:

$$\text{R.O.C.E.} = \frac{£32,000}{£191,000} \times 100$$
$$= 16 \cdot 7\%$$

The percentage for the previous year is 15·9 per cent showing a modest improvement in management's performance in its use of total assets.

Alternatively R.O.C.E. is measured by the fraction:

$$\frac{\text{Net profit before tax and interest}}{\text{Net capital employed (net assets)}}$$

The reader will notice that the denominator is different and includes only longer-term funds employed in the business. Thus short-term liabilities, such as creditors, are excluded since they are used for short periods only before they are paid and replaced. However, a business that effectively uses short-term funds such as trade creditors, and bank overdraft as long-term sources should regard these funds as semi-permanent and include them in the denominator when calculating R.O.C.E.

8. Return on investment. This measures the return on the proprietor's investment in the company, being their total share capital plus the reserves that they indirectly own. Naturally they are interested in the profits available for distribution, *i.e.* the post-tax profit figure.

$$\text{R.O.I.} = \frac{\text{Profits after tax}}{\text{Total share capital plus reserves}} \times 100$$

In this case the post-tax profit figure accruing to the share-holders in 1976 is £16,000, *i.e.*:

$$= \frac{£16,000}{£135,000} \times 100$$
$$= 11 \cdot 8\%: \text{ again, a modest improvement over the preceding year's figure of } 11 \cdot 5\%.$$

It is possible to develop the concept of R.O.I. further and

to calculate the return on the investment contributed by each class of proprietor.

(a) Return on proprietors' equity investment.

$$= \frac{\text{Net profit accruing to ordinary shareholders}}{\text{Ordinary share capital} + \text{reserves}}$$

$$= 1976 \frac{£16,000 - £1,000 \text{ Preference dividend}}{£125,000}$$

$$= 12\%$$

(b) Return on proprietors' preference investment.

$$= \frac{\text{Net profit accruing to the preference shareholders}}{\text{Preference share capital}}$$

$$= 1976 \frac{£1,000}{£10,000}$$

$$= 10\%$$

In this case, the return on *preference capital* is that stipulated in the terms under which these shares are issued. However, their R.O.I. could be less than 10 per cent if net profits are inadequate to cover their dividend. Alternatively, it could be greater than 10 per cent if the shares are *participating preference* which entitle them to their fixed dividend plus an extra dividend out of remaining profits when the ordinary shareholders are paid.

9. Margins on sales. These measure the mark-up on cost of sales and therefore the degree of protection to profits arising from inflationary trends in costs. The first ratio: gross profits to sales, measures the efficiency of management in converting materials into sales.

$$\frac{\text{Gross profit}}{\text{Sales}} \times 100$$

$$= 1976 \frac{£45,000}{£245,000} \times 100$$

$$= 18 \cdot 4\% : 1975 = 17 \cdot 4\%$$

Naturally the highest possible profit mark-up is preferred but the limiting factor will always be customers' reactions and competitors' marketing policies if sales prices are raised in an attempt to increase the margin.

The second margin relates net profit to sales, *i.e.* it is the income remaining after charging all indirect expenses and is an excellent indication of the efficiency of management in controlling such costs.

$$\frac{\text{Net profit}}{\text{Sales}} \times 100$$
$$= 1976 \; \frac{\text{£}31,000}{\text{£}245,000}$$
$$= 12{\cdot}6\% : 1975 = 12{\cdot}1\%$$

ACTIVITY

10. Activity. Company accounts contain information that indicate the activity level or, specifically, how effectively the company uses its resources.

11. Sales revenue. This figure found in the Trading and Profit and Loss Account indicates how successful the company has been in generating income. In isolation it is of limited value, although the trend in sales revenue can be established when comparisons are made with the previous year's figures.

12. Movements in assets. Changes in the value of assets should be inspected and any significant movements in items noted and the cause discovered. For example, stocks may have risen disproportionally to other assets, with the result that too much working capital is tied up. However, caution is needed for, on the other hand, the company could have adopted different distribution arrangements, e.g. direct selling which requires higher stock levels because the company is itself performing the wholesale function; or it could be in the process of building up stocks of a new product or model in anticipation of its launch. Similarly the cause of higher debtor figures should be investigated and credit control tightened if the cause is non-payment by debtors rather than a deliberate policy of credit extention by the organisation.

13. The activity ratios. These are the best measures of showing how effective the organisation has been in using the resources under its control. They relate the various asset items to the sales revenue figure, measuring the asset turnover, i.e. how many times an asset item has been turned over to generate the sales revenue figure. Naturally the higher the turnover the greater the efficiency in using these scarce resources.

14. Stock turnover. This is calculated as follows:

$$\text{Stock turnover} = \frac{\text{Sales revenue}}{\text{Stocks}}$$

and in the case of the Lemming Company Ltd. is:

$$\frac{£245,000}{£46,000}$$

$$= 5 \cdot 3 \text{ for 1976 and } 5 \cdot 7 \text{ for 1975}$$

The lower turnover figure reveals that the Company was less successful in 1976 in utilising its stocks. Expressed in a slightly different way, this means that 18·8p worth of stock was needed to generate £1 worth of sales $\left(i.e. \dfrac{£46,000}{£245,000}\right)$ and only 17·4p in 1975.

There are two points worth mentioning. Firstly there is a case for averaging the stock figure for use as the denominator (*i.e.* opening stocks + closing stocks ÷ 2), because stocks are measured at one point in time whereas the sales revenue accrues over the financial period. Seasonality of sales, or an expanding or contracting sales trend, adds weight for the use of adjusted stock figures. Secondly, "cost of sales" figures could be employed as numerator which would then make sales directly comparable with stock values which are measured at cost.

Thus in this example the stock turnover (*i.e.* how quickly stocks are converted into sales) can be calculated as follows:

$$\text{Stock turnover} = \frac{\text{Cost of sales}}{\text{Average stock of goods held}}$$

$$= \frac{£200,000}{(£40,000 + £46,000) \div 2}$$

$$= 4 \cdot 6 \text{ times in the year}$$

Naturally a high turnover figure means that there is less risk to the company if there is a fall in the market price of the goods.

The raw material turnover ratio is calculated as follows:

$$\frac{\text{Cost of materials used}}{\text{Average stocks of raw materials}}$$

15. Debtors' turnover. This measures the number of times that debtors' balances are turned over to secure the sales revenue.

$$\text{Debtors' turnover} = \frac{\text{Sales revenue}}{\text{debtors}}$$

$$= 1976 \ \frac{£245,000}{£65,000} = 3\cdot8$$

$$1975 \ \frac{£230,000}{£52,000} = 4\cdot4$$

However, an alternative method of measuring the effectiveness of debtors' control is to calculate the time it takes on average for debtors to pay for their purchases. Sales revenue is divided by the number of days in the year (conventionally 360) and this sales per day figure is in turn divided into the debtors' total.

Sales per day   c.f. Purchase per day

$$= 1976 \ \frac{£245,000}{360} = £680 \qquad \frac{£100,000}{360} = £278$$

$$1975 \ \frac{£230,000}{360} = £638 \qquad \frac{95,000}{360} = £263$$

Assume purchases are 50% of cost of sales

Average collection period   Average payment period

$$= \frac{\text{Debtors}}{\text{Sales per day}} \qquad\qquad = \frac{\text{Creditors}}{\text{Purchases per day}}$$

$$= 1976 \ \frac{£65,000}{£680} = 96 \text{ days} \qquad = 1976 \ \frac{£28,000}{£278} = 100 \text{ days}$$

$$1975 \ \frac{£52,000}{£638} = 81 \text{ days} \qquad 1975 \ \frac{30,000}{£263} = 114 \text{ days}$$

16. Current asset turnover. This ratio of sales revenue to total current assets measures how effective management is in controlling the more liquid assets.

$$\text{Current asset turnover} = \frac{\text{Sales revenue}}{\text{Current assets}}$$

$$= 1976 \ \frac{£245,000}{£111,000} = 2\cdot2 \qquad 1975 \ \frac{£230,000}{£97,000} = 2\cdot4$$

17. Fixed asset turnover. This activity ratio measures the turnover of all capital assets including land, building, plant and machinery, furniture and fittings, motor vehicles, etc., although for a detailed analysis the turnover of each category of fixed asset could be calculated.

$$\text{Fixed asset turnover} = \frac{\text{Sales revenue}}{\text{Fixed assets}}$$

$$= 1976 \frac{£245,000}{£80,000} = 3 \cdot 1 \qquad 1975 \frac{£230,000}{£85,000} = 2 \cdot 7$$

18. Total asset turnover. This is calculated as follows:

$$\text{Total asset turnover} = \frac{\text{Sales revenue}}{\text{Total assets}}$$

$$= 1976 \frac{£245,000}{£191,000} = 1 \cdot 28 \qquad 1975 \frac{£230,000}{£182,000} = 1 \cdot 26$$

These activity ratios reveal that 1976 was a slight improvement on 1975 and that the company had generated a larger volume of sales revenue from its total investment of assets.

SOLVENCY

19. Solvency. Solvency means the ability of the company to pay its debts. Assuming that the assets of Lemming Co. Ltd. shown previously are valued realistically then the company is clearly solvent, *i.e.* if all assets are sold then the proceeds are more than sufficient to meet the claims of the debenture holders and creditors.

Liquidity is a closely related concept that measures the ability of the company to find cash to meet maturing obligations. Nevertheless, it is quite possible for a company to fail if it cannot raise sufficient cash funds to meet immediate debts even though it is solvent in that total assets (when realised) match total debts.

20. Value of assets not charged. Land has for long been regarded as suitable collateral for borrowing since it tends to appreciate and thereby offers the creditor a high degree of safety. Therefore a comparison between a company's fixed assets, particularly land, and the Register of Charges will reveal what assets are free of liens or charges of creditors and available if required as collateral for further borrowing.

21. The company's borrowing powers. These powers and

borrowing limits are set out in the Memorandum and Articles of Association.

22. The authorised capital. In the case of Lemming Co. Ltd. the authorised share capital is 150,000 £1 shares, of which 100,000 have been issued. This means that the Company could issue a further 50,000 shares should it require additional capital.

23. Value of net current assets. The net current assets figure is the difference between total current assets and total current liabilities. Thus the figures for 1976 and 1975 in an example are £68,000 (£111,000 − £43,000) and £57,000 (£97,000 − £40,000) respectively. It shows the margin of safety between the company's assets and those debts coming up for repayment, and is one of the most important measures of solvency and the ability of the company to continue trading.

24. Estimates of contingent liabilities. This liability becomes payable upon the happening of an event, *e.g.* a court decision goes against the company at which time liquid funds must be found to settle the liability. An example is found in the Balance Sheet of Lemming Co. Ltd.

25. Current ratio. The current ratio is the conventional measure that shows whether a company can meet its short-term liabilities out of the assets that are realised into cash within the same time scale.

$$\text{Current ratio} = \frac{\text{Current assets}}{\text{Current liabilities}}$$

$$= 1976 \, \frac{£111,000}{£43,000} = 2{\cdot}58 \qquad 1975 \, \frac{£97,000}{£40,000} = 2{\cdot}42$$

These ratios show that the Lemming Co. Ltd. had a higher margin of safety in 1976 to deal with any fluctuations that may occur in cash flow.

The informed manager who fears that sales turnover is increasing too quickly in relation to working capital, *i.e.* over-trading could be occurring, can confirm this by calculating the current ratio and the ratio of creditors to debtors. If the latter figure is increasing while the former is falling then there is indication of overtrading; the shortage of cash forcing the organisation to finance trade through credit and loans. The consequences are serious and could, if credit became tight, affect the security of the shareholders' investment, employees' wages and creditors' debts and therefore demand immediate investigation to identify the cause and remedial measures.

26. Quick ratio or "acid test." This ratio of liquidity is similar to the current ratio except that stocks, the least liquid of current assets, are eliminated. Thus the quick ratio tests the ability of the company to pay off its immediate debts out of its most liquid assets.

$$\text{Quick ratio} = \frac{\text{Current assets} - \text{stocks}}{\text{Current liabilities}}$$
$$= 1976 \frac{£65,000}{£43,000} = 1 \cdot 5 \qquad 1975 \frac{£57,000}{£40,000} = 1 \cdot 42$$

27. Average collection period. This has already been calculated (*see* 15) as ninety-six days in 1976 compared with eighty-one days in 1975. Obviously these figures should be compared with the terms of sales, and a policy of tight credit control implemented if the average collection period is significantly longer than the credit terms.

GEARING AND CAPITAL STRUCTURE

28. Gearing and capital structure. Creditors and shareholders have a conflict of interest and consequently have different views on the ideal capital structure. Creditors firstly require some degree of security and prefer that shareholders have a substantial stake in the company's total capital. Shareholders on the other hand may prefer to control the company through a small share capital and raise additional capital by means of non-voting debenture and loan capital to take advantage of capital gearing. This means that if the company can earn 18 per cent on capital when interest rates are 10 per cent, it pays the shareholders to finance additional capital through loans and to retain 8 per cent profit for themselves.

29. Redemption dates. If a company has already issued fixed interest or dividend securities then its room for manoeuvre is obviously more limited than one that has relied exclusively on ordinary share capital. However, if these securities have been issued with a fairly wide time-span, then the company may redeem and replace with lower interest rates when market rates are lower. Information regarding these redemption dates and classes of share and loan capital is contained in the Memorandum and Articles and Balance Sheet.

30. Debt ratio. The debt ratio measures the ratio of total funds contributed by creditors. The conflict of interest referred to in **28** implies that creditors prefer a low ratio and shareholders a high figure. A low figure will cushion the creditor against losses in the event of winding up, while a high debt ratio benefits the owners in terms of gearing and control.

$$\text{Debt ratio} = \frac{\text{Total debt}}{\text{Total assets}}.$$

$$= 1976 \frac{£56,000}{£191,000} = 29\% \qquad 1975 \frac{£52,000}{£182,000} = 28\%$$

Thus we see that in Lemming Co. Ltd., the creditors have little to fear on the above score. Generally they will not want their debt to exceed the total investments of shareholders; in fact their debt is very safely covered.

A related measurement of the degree of protection afforded to a lender by an asset is the *asset cover*, *i.e.* the number of times the asset covers the loan. Thus if, in an example, the debenture of £10,000 is secured on the land and building valued at £60,000, then the cover is six, which appears to be safe, especially so if the land is undervalued.

31. Interest cover. This shows the extent to which earnings can fall and still cover fixed interest charges. Naturally a high margin of safety is preferred. A low interest cover figure could be serious because a bad trading period resulting in non-payment of interest could result in the creditors petitioning for winding up and the repayment of their debts.

$$\text{Interest cover} = \frac{\text{Profit before tax and interest}}{\text{Interest charge}}$$

$$= 1976 \frac{£32,000}{£1,000} = 32 \qquad 1975 \frac{£29,000}{£1,000} = 29$$

Thus interest payments are well covered in both years.

32. Net worth: fixed assets. Shareholders should have a substantial contribution in the total capital employed. It is considered desirable for them to contribute funds that finance all fixed assets and a proportion of current assets.

$$\frac{\text{Net worth}}{\text{Fixed assets}} = 1976 \; \frac{£135,000}{£80,000} = 1.69 \quad 1975 \; \frac{£130,000}{£85,000} = 1.53$$

Thus shareholders have contributed the whole of fixed assets and the majority of current assets.

33. Gearing factor. This factor measures the relative proportion of the types of capital employed in a company. For example:

$$\text{Gearing factor} = \frac{\text{Loan capital and preference share capital}}{\text{Ordinary share capital}}$$
$$= 1976 \; \frac{£20,000}{£100,000} = 20\% \quad 1975 = 20\%$$

Thus in both years preference shareholders and debenture holders have contributed a small proportion in comparison with ordinary shareholders.

Another way of looking at gearing is to express borrowings of all kinds as a percentage of the equity base. The essence of gearing lies in keeping a balance between these, recognising that while shareholders may benefit, the interest is a prior charge on the profits of the company, and the higher the borrowings, the more vulnerable is the company in the event of a decline in its profits.

TABLE VIII – CAPITAL GEARING PERCENTAGES
(LEMMING CO.)

		1975	1976
Borrowings:	Overdraft	—	£5,000
	Debentures	£10,000	£10,000
	Preference Shares	£10,000	£10,000
	Total	£20,000	£25,000
Equity		£120,000	£125,000
	Gearing %	16·6%	20%

Table VIII shows that gearing has increased in 1976 from 16·6 per cent to 20 per cent which means that for every £1 of ordinary shareholders' funds in the business, the company has 116·6p and 20p respectively. (*See* Table VIII for the effects of gearing on dividends.)

OWNERSHIP AND CONTROL

34. Ownership. The final criterion for examining and interpreting company accounts is ownership.

35. Secured creditors. If the porportion of secured assets is small in relation to total assets then ownership is unaffected. However, as the proportion increases the company's freedom of action is reduced so that secured creditors may become in effect controllers.

36. Shareholders' interests. The Register of Shareholders' Interests records those shareholders holding 10 per cent or more of share capital. A significant holding of a class share capital possession voting rights gives the shareholder a degree of influence and perhaps control in company affairs. Examination of the voting rights of the classes of share capital can be revealing, *e.g.* preference shares may have no voting rights except if dividends are in arrears.

37. Vote-gearing.

(*a*) For example, the vote-gearing of Lemming Co. Ltd. with issued capital of 100,000 £1 ordinary shares (with full voting rights) and 10,000 £1 preference shares, plus 10,000 £1 debentures (without voting rights) is:

$$\frac{\text{Total capital}}{\text{Total voting capital}} = \frac{£100,000 + 10,000 + 10,000}{£100,000} = 1·2$$

Here ordinary shareholders control capital 1·2 times their own nominal capital.

(*b*) However, vote-gearing of ordinary shareholders is tempered if similar voting rights are given to the preference shareholders, for example:

$$\frac{£100,000 + 10,000 + 10,000}{£100,000 + 10,000} = 1·09$$

USE OF RATIOS

38. Value of ratios. We have already established that absolute figures can be misleading when assessing company performance; ratios, however, enable us to summarise and clarify
information and throw up inter-relationships. The following
general rules apply in the use of ratios:

(*a*) Compilation should be speedy.

(*b*) Compilation is costly, and only those of direct application should be compiled. However, as staff become con-
versant with their construction and application, ratio
analysis may be developed further.

(*c*) Ratios should be presented in the most appropriate
manner for the organisation.

(*d*) Ratios do not give financial control but pin-point areas
for investigation.

(*e*) Ratios should not be used in isolation, *e.g.* if sales
increase by 6 per cent per year, and profits by 3 per cent,
this apparently satisfactory situation is proved otherwise
if this is achieved by the injection of a larger amount of
capital. Therefore ratios become more meaningful when
compared with others. Comparison may be made within
the organisation and is described as *trend analysis*, or with
other firms in the industry or industry generally. This latter
form of comparison is termed *comparative analysis*.

Throughout this chapter we have used *trend analysis* in
assessing the performance of Lemming Co. Ltd., *i.e.* direct
comparisons between 1976 and 1975 to establish whether
Lemming Co. Ltd. is improving or deteriorating. The remainder of the chapter will deal with *comparative analysis*.

39. Comparative Analysis. There are a number of sources of
ratio statistics available to companies. Trade associations and
the Centre for Inter-Firm Comparisons, among others, supply
subscribers with detailed ratios indicating the range of performance of constituent firms, with often a comment on the
subscribers' strengths and weaknesses. Statistics within the
following areas are of considerable value for companies wishing
to compare their performance with other companies:

(*a*) *Return on assets.*

(b) *Profit on sales.*

(c) *Sales to capital employed on operating assets* showing how much capital is "tied up" to achieve these sales.

(d) *Stocks to sales.* This shows how many weeks of stocks are carried to maintain current sales. Naturally the length of the manufacturing cycle and material supply delivery situation are considerations in setting stock levels, but as a general rule industry will aim to have approximately two months' stocks.

(e) *Debtors to sales.* The average length of time for customers to pay invoices is six weeks. If this figure is exceeded then it represents tied up funds that cannot be used unless invoice discounting facilities are used.

(f) *Current assets to current liabilities.* The generally accepted rule of thumb ratio is 2:1. However, this should be interpreted with caution since much depends on the characteristics of the industry, *e.g.* normal seasonality of trade may require excessive stock levels with obvious deteriorations in the ratio.

(g) *Quick assets to current liabilities.* The acid test's generally accepted norm is 1:1.

(h) *Advertising costs to sales.*

(i) *Production costs to sales.* If this increases, then the profit margin must deteriorate and the cause should be investigated.

(j) *Administration costs to sales.*

(k) *Distribution costs to sales.*

40. Use of investment ratios. In the post-war period, a number of investment ratios have been used as the yardsticks of investment performance. They are:

(a) Dividend and earning yields in the 1950s.

(b) Price/earnings ratio after the introduction of corporation tax in 1965. This means that if a company's share price is (£1) and post-corporation tax earnings are (10p) per share, then the P/E ratio is 10:1, or 10. Thus the share price (£1) represents ten times the last annual earnings or, put another way, the investor will recoup his capital investment in ten years, if earnings are unchanged.

Companies with good prospects of high future earnings were

commanded a high P/E ratio and offered the investor a hedge against inflation.

(c) In the 1970s the rate of inflation overtook the antici-pated rate of earnings, and with the added confusions of the imputation system of corporation tax in 1973 investors' attention turned to the following:

(i) *Liquidity ratios.* The very high cost of money meant that companies should be self-financing as far as possible. Alternatively, trade credit should be used when cheaper than loans. Examples are the quick ratio and stocks to creditors' ratio (say, 60 per cent) respectively.

(ii) *Dividend and earning yields.* With the very high yields on fixed interest stock (15 per cent May 1974) attention once more reverted to comparative yields on equities.

PROGRESS TEST 8

1. For what reasons are people interested in published accounts? (1–2)

2. Distinguish between R.O.C.E. and R.O.I. (7–8)

3. What ratios measure a company's utilisation of assets? (10–18)

4. Explain the following:
    (a) current ratio;
    (b) acid test;
    (c) gearing. (19–33)

5. Distinguish between trend and comparative analysis. (38–39)

6. For what reasons have the yardsticks for investment appraisal changed since the war? (40)

CHAPTER IX

ACCOUNTING FOR INFLATION

WHAT IS INFLATION?

1. Definition. Inflation can be simply defined as a general rise in prices usually as a result of "too much money chasing too few goods." This is certainly true of specific commodities, and confirmed by the motorists' experiences in November 1973. With the cut-back in supplies of oil by O.P.E.C. members, a run on garages ensued which led to unofficial rationing by garages. In a free market this immediately would have resulted in higher prices for petrol and there were in fact recorded cases of garages taking advantage of the excessive demand by doubling or trebling the price of petrol.

Thus excessive purchasing power causes higher prices for specific goods. Furthermore, the general price level of all goods tends to rise when total purchasing power is in excess of total available goods.

2. Types of inflation. Two broad types of inflation can be distinguished:

(*a*) *Cost push.* This occurs when there is a shortage of materials or labour (known by economists as factors of production). Consequently, the prices or costs of these factors tend to rise and producers pass on these higher costs to the end user. In other words retail prices are *pushed up* by the inflated costs of production.

(*b*) *Demand pull.* This arises when total purchasing power is increasing faster than available goods and services. Excessive demand by consumers *pulls up* prices for goods and services generally. This excessive demand is caused by:

(*i*) Earnings increasing faster than output of goods and services.

132

(*ii*) A high rate of credit expansion by banks and hire purchase companies.

These two types of inflation exist concurrently. They inter-
act to generate an inflationary spiral of wages and prices, as
when excess demand leads to a higher cost of living and the
inevitable wage claims. Manufacturers then pass these on by
way of higher prices, to complete the vicious circle.

3. Changes in retail prices. One useful indicator of the
change in prices and thereby the cost of living is the monthly
General Index of Retail Prices or Retail Price Index (R.P.I.).
This provides a "running commentary" of price changes by
measuring the month to month movements of representative
shopping basket items bought by the general public. These
items consist of the following:

(*a*) Food.
(*b*) Alcoholic drink.
(*c*) Tobacco.
(*d*) Housing.
(*e*) Fuel and light.
(*f*) Durable household goods.
(*g*) Clothing and footwear.
(*h*) Transport and vehicles.
(*i*) Miscellaneous goods.
(*j*) Services.
(*k*) Meals outside the home.

About 150,000 separate price quotations for these goods and
services are used every month in compiling this index.

Clearly, certain items are relatively more important, in that
a larger proportion of the housekeeping budget is expended
on them. Thus food, housing, transport and vehicles are
allocated a higher weighting than, say, services and meals
outside the home; changes in their costs have a significant
effect on the index. For a full description of the index the
reader should see *Method of Construction and Calculation of the
Index of Retail Prices* (H.M.S.O.).

4. Average annual changes in retail prices. The average
annual changes in retail prices are summarised in Table IX:

TABLE IX.—AVERAGE ANNUAL CHANGES IN RETAIL PRICES
(1920–70).

1920–30	− 3·0% p.a.
1930–40	− 0·5%
1940–50	+ 7·5%
1950–60	+ 4·2%
1960–70	+ 4·8%
1970–73	+ 11·0%

Examination of the table shows that annual retail prices
fell in the depression of the 1920s and 1930s but increased after
1940. Since 1970 the rate of inflation in retail prices is historic-
ally high and the R.P.I. reveals the following trend:

TABLE X.—CHANGE IN RETAIL PRICE INDEX (1970–74).

Jan. 1970	base 100
1971	113·2
1972	121·2
1973	132·4
1974	141·5

Clearly as prices go up, the amount that can be bought
with a given amount of money goes down in proportion: in
real terms the purchasing power of the pound within the U.K.
has fallen since 1940 and substantially since 1970.

EFFECTS OF INFLATION

5. Effects of inflation. While a moderate degree of inflation
may be desirable as it tends to be associated with expansion
and may stimulate business activity, excessive price increases
produce the following problems:

(a) *People lose confidence in money.* Because of the declin-
ing value of money they are less willing to save. Furthermore, they may spend all of their income since they know
that money will be worth less in the future. Thus purchasing
power increases, causing further price increases.

(b) *The reduction in savings* checks investment and
economic growth.

(c) *Exports become less competitive*; imports are relatively cheaper and more attractive so that deficits are incurred on the balance of payments. Consequently the currency comes under pressure in foreign exchange markets.

(d) *Inflation tends to redistribute income* to the detriment of those on fixed incomes (*e.g.* pensioners and holders of fixed interest stocks), yet to the short-run advantage of profit and wage earners. Similarly, debtors will gain at the expense of creditors. Every house buyer knows this. By contracting to buy a house today valued at £15,000 in 1974 pounds with repayments spread over, say, 25 years one is in fact repaying the fixed debt with depreciating pounds; in addition, this inflation psychology generates additional demand for houses and hence higher house values, so that by 1999 the house may be worth many times its 1974 value.

(e) *Currency may become worthless* in hyper-inflation as in Germany in 1923. Savings are destroyed.

INFLATION AND ACCOUNTS

6. Inflation and economic progress. Statistics of national income show that the U.K.'s gross domestic product (*i.e.* the total value of goods and services produced in one year) was £100 million in 1970. In 1973 it was £109·7 million. However, we know that a 1973 pound was worth less than a 1970 pound, so that to measure true economic progress (*i.e.* the real increase in output of goods and services in the U.K.) we must discount inflation and measure 1973's output at 1970 prices. Thus we compare like with like.

	1970	1971	1972	1973
Gross domestic product (g.d.p.) (at 1970 prices)	100	101·4	104·1	109·7

However, this logic and common sense is not applied to company accounts. Company accounts record transactions at the time of the transactions in terms of the money values at that time. A company's Balance Sheets may show that it has grown by 10 per cent during the year. However, this apparently satisfactory position is reversed if one is told that inflation over the year has been 10 per cent. In fact, the company has not grown at all. One can imagine a more complex example. Imagine that a company incorporated in 1970 uses shareholders funds to buy land and buildings, plant is bought in

1971 with 1971 pounds, materials bought with 1972 pounds and labour hired with 1973 pounds. This generates sales revenue and profits measured in 1974 pounds. Clearly these company accounts fail to give a "true and fair" view of the economic progress and the firm's general trading and financial position. Furthermore, the distortions between what is recorded and what is real widens as the rate of inflation increases.

7. Inflation and replacement of assets. A very serious consequence of inflation is that companies may find that they have set aside insufficient funds to replace exhausted assets.

Depreciation is a charge against profits that retains funds within the company, and in theory, funds equal to the total depreciation provisions are available to replace the depreciating assets. However, inflation means that each asset now costs more to replace; consequently, either the asset is not replaced or additional funds must be raised to meet the short-fall. This is illustrated graphically in Fig. 36.

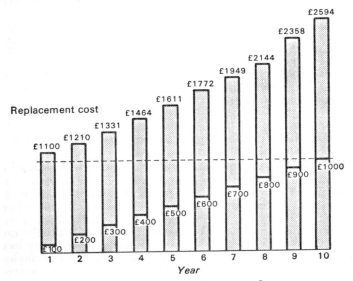

FIG. 36.—Inflation and replacement of assets.

The assumptions underlying Fig. 36 are:

(a) Original cost is £1,000.

(b) Expected life of asset is ten years.

(c) Depreciation is on a straight line basis: i.e. £100 p.a. for ten years.

(d) Anticipated rate of inflation is 10 per cent.

Examination of Fig. 36 shows that depreciation based on historical cost (the original purchase price of the asset) fails to set aside sufficient funds for the replacement of the asset. In fact, at a rate of inflation of 10 per cent the total short-fall amounts to £1,594 (£2,594 − £1,000).

8. How inflation distorts accounts. Inflation tends to distort the picture of the company's performance and financial structure in several ways:

(a) *Assets are under-valued.* If management fails to re-value assets regularly, then the Balance Sheet understates the true worth of the company and leads to the classic take-over situation. For example, let us assume that the example below represents the worth of a company based on the original cost of its assets. After allowing for debts to outsiders, there remains £80,000 shared among the 50,000 shares (£1·60 per share).

However, if the assets are now valued at market price, then the value of the shareholders interest is £100,000 or £2·00 per share. Clearly the company's share price will be below its true value while the company values assets on original cost: anybody knowing their market value could offer to buy shares cheaply at a price in excess of £1·60 and up to £2·00 each.

		Historical cost	*Market value*
Total assets		£88,000	£108,000
Less: Loan capital	£3,000		
current liabilities	5,000	8,000	8,000
Value of shareholders' interest (50,000 £1 shares issued)		£80,000	100,000
Value of one share	=	80,000	100,000
		50,000	50,000
	=	£1·60	£2·00

(b) *Profits are exaggerated.* We have seen in Fig. 36 that depreciation, the notional charge against profits, tends to be too low in times of inflation when based on original cost on assets. This results in the following:

(i) Profits tend to be overstated.

(ii) This leads to underpricing of products.

(iii) The company fails to retain sufficient funds for the replacement of assets and is eventually forced to raise additional capital to maintain the real value of assets.

(iv) The company has not charged revenue with the full economic cost of using the assets (by means of depreciation in the Profit and Loss Account).

(c) *High geared companies gain.* Companies financing assets by borrowing money gain over self-financing companies. This is because the monetary debt depreciates in inflation, *i.e.* £100 borrowed in 1966 and repayable say in 1972 involves the payment of the fixed amount £100 which in reality is worth only £71 (*see* below):

TABLE XI.—PURCHASING POWER OF THE POUND.

1872	100										
1900	115½	100									
1913	106½	92	100								
1920	42½	37	40	100							
1938	68	59	64	159½	100						
1946	40	35	38	94½	59	100					
1956	25½	22½	24	60½	38	64	100				
1966	19½	17	18½	46	28½	48½	76	100			
1970	16	14	15½	38	24	40½	63½	83	100		
1971	15	13	14	35	22	37	58	76	91½	100	
1972	14	12	13	32½	20½	34½	54	71	85½	93½	100
1973	12½	11	12	29½	18½	31½	49	65	78	85½	91½

Source: The British Economy in Figures (Lloyds Bank).

9. Replacement cost accounting. One solution to the inflation problem is replacement cost accounting. This means that a company adopting this method of accounting would adjust its accounts in the following ways:

(a) Fixed assets are revalued in the Balance Sheet at the current price of replacement.

(b) The anticipated life of the asset is estimated and the appropriate amount of depreciation charged against profits.

(c) Stocks are revalued at replacement value.

	(i) Conventional cost	(ii) Replacement cost
Cost of sales bought in 1975	£5,000	£6,000
Sales 1976	6,000	6,000
Gross profit	1,000	—
Less: Depreciation	100	120
Profit	900	(120)
Fixed assets	1,000	1,200
Less: Depreciation 10%	100	120
	£900	£1,080

Extracts from Balance Sheet and Profit and Loss Account

In the above example, (i) summarises Balance Sheet and Profit and Loss Account items in conventional cost form. Opening stocks cost £5,000 and are sold for £6,000 one year later. Conventionally profits are £1,000. Furthermore, if fixed assets are £1,000 at cost and 10 per cent depreciation is charged each year, then £100 is charged against profit reducing it to £900.

In Column (ii) opening stocks are valued at replacement cost, *i.e.* £6,000. Similarly, fixed assets are revalued at £1,200 and the higher depreciation charge of £120 charged to the Profit and Loss Account. Consequently a loss of £120 is incurred as opposed to the profit of £900 under the conventional costing system.

If assets are revalued annually at replacement cost, then the Balance Sheet can be said to reflect more accurately a "true and fair" view of the companies financial situation. Furthermore, the higher depreciation charges reduce profits to a more realistic level, and ensure that depreciation provisions are eventually adequate for asset replacement. From the economists' point of view, it is important that depreciation reflects the economic cost of employing the resources; replacement cost accounting satisfies this requirement.

10. Price level accounting. This method goes further than replacement cost accounting in that all Profit and Loss and Balance Sheet items are adjusted. Furthermore, it overcomes a basic weakness of the replacement costing method which fails to make true profit comparisons over time. In other words, after applying the replacement cost method net profits may be £10,000 in 1970 and still £10,000 in 1973. This is surely unsatisfactory in an inflationary situation and requires a general price level adjustment in order to appraise its economic performance.

Central to the price level accounting method and means of adjustment is a *consumer price index*. The official C.P.I. is published by the Central Statistical Office and measures annual changes in the purchasing power of the pound.

11. Advantages of using a consumer price index.

(*a*) Inflation is a general increase in prices, and a general price index deflator applied to inflated values will show real changes from a base year.

(*b*) It measures the effects of general price increases which is appropriate to any business.

(*c*) It represents a well-established, suitable standard for all companies.

An example of price level accounting is given below.

PROFIT AND LOSS ACCOUNT FOR 1974

Conventional form			Adjustments		Adjusted for inflation
Sales Revenue		£10,000	$£10,000 \times \frac{110^1}{105} =$		£10,476
Less: Costs	£5,000		$£5,000 \times \frac{110^1}{105} =$	£5,238	
Depreciation £2,000		7,000	$£10,000 \times \frac{110^2}{95} = £11,578 \div 5$		7,553
				$= £2,315$	
Trading Profits		3,000			2,923
Less: Interest		500	$500 \times \frac{110^1}{105} =$		524
Net Profits		2,500			2,399
Less: Monetary loss[3]		—			100
Adjusted net profit		£2,500			£2,299

FIG. 37.—An example of price level accounting.

Typical C.P.I. numbers
Year ended 1972 = 95
Year ended 1973 = 100
Year ended 1974 = 110
Average 1974 = 105

1. Sales revenue or cost $\times \dfrac{\text{Year end Index 1974}}{\text{Average Index 1974}}$
2. Assume asset is bought in 1972 for £10,000 and written off at 20% over five years.
3. This represents the difference between the losses incurred in owning assets expressed in monetary terms and the gains from liabilities expressed in monetary terms.

Assume (*i*) Current asset; Jan. 1974 bank balance	£2,000
Adjusted value = £2,000 $\times \dfrac{110}{100}$ =	2,200
Dec. 1974 bank balance	2,000
Loss	£200
(*ii*) Liability; Jan. 1974 loan	1,000
Adjusted value = £1,000 $\times \dfrac{110}{100}$ =	1,100
Dec. 1974 loan	1,000
Gain	£100

Monetary loss = £200 − £100 = £100

This example is not intended to illustrate a comprehensive treatment of inflation accounting but to emphasise the following points:

(*a*) The general relationship between conventional accounting form and price level accounting.

(*b*) The manner in which typical C.P.I. numbers are applied to sales revenue and costs to remove the effects of general inflation as defined by the C.P.I. index.

(*c*) To appreciate that companies, like individuals, gain and lose from inflation (have a monetary loss since the depreciating bank balance outweighs the appreciating loan).

12. The future of accounting inflation. In 1973 the Accounting Standards Steering Committee suggested a way of standardising practice in inflation accounting. Their recommendation was based on a general purchasing power standard, *i.e.* the C.P.I. The seriousness of these suggestions implies advantages for inflation accounting. The advantages of inflation accounting are as follows:

(*a*) Shareholders can see whether their investments have grown in real terms.

(*b*) Management can see the true profit levels and pursue a realistic pricing policy.

(*c*) Management can relate dividends to the real ability of the company to pay dividends. With dividends, constrained management can augment and match resources with capital requirements. As a result fewer external injections of cash are required.

(*d*) The economy benefits if companies generally make efficient use of resources.

However, despite these advantages and the moves to promote discussion on a suitable price accounting system, there are still a number of problems to be overcome.

13. Problems associated with inflation accounting.

(*a*) Taxation rates need to be changed assuming that the government requires the same tax yield. This is because company earnings would fall perhaps by as much as 20 per cent overall.

(*b*) It would officially recognise inflation and might deepen the inflationary psychology and cause inflation to accelerate.

(*c*) Companies might demand depreciation tax allowances on replacement cost and not original cost. This would require a considerable preparation.

(*d*) Companies might accelerate inflationary pressures by pursuing high price policies in an attempt to beat inflation.

PROGRESS TEST 9

1. Define inflation and illustrate its effects on company accounts. (1–8)

2. Show how inflation distorts company performances. (8–9)

PART THREE

MONEY: HOW TO CONTROL IT AND PLAN FOR PROFIT

In this section we consider the need for effective controls and examine some control techniques that managers can use to improve their performance in securing predetermined objectives. Generally the manager's objectives are defined by his budget, for this expresses in financial or quantitative terms a plan which he should implement and control over the appropriate time span in order to achieve the desired level of performance for that part of the organisation for which he is responsible. Hence the expression that managers should *control to plan* so that managers' activities interlock and thereby achieve the target set by top management for the overall organisation.

Furthermore, on the assumption that managers who control should also participate in the formulating of plans, this section examines certain techniques that have general application in the profit planning stage in the areas of cost reduction, capital expenditure and production policy.

CHAPTER X

MONEY: WHO IS RESPONSIBLE FOR IT?

RESPONSIBILITY ACCOUNTING

1. Definition. The reader–manager drawing upon his own experience will undoubtedly agree that managers must be forward-looking: some form of plan is vital to provide the company, its department managers and staff with a purpose and strength of motivation. Failure to anticipate events and formulate a policy inevitably results in a crisis atmosphere with unnecessary strains and pressures on staff and an unsatisfactory company performance.

Management, therefore, should be concerned with setting objectives for the organisation and devising the necessary plans to achieve these goals. Obviously, this means setting targets for all constituent parts of the organisation. Furthermore, managers who participate in advising on departmental or functional targets and in the setting of appropriate standards or budgets, should be responsible for the control of the day-to-day operations and the securing of these targets. This is a description of responsibility accounting which may be defined as the process of quantifying the manager's work, and the application of positive and constructive control systems so that managers can meet their objectives.

2. Principles of control. Control, defined as "the regulation of activities to secure predetermined objectives," has three elements:

    (*a*) The determination of the objectives.
    (*b*) Comparison between the objective and actual performance.
    (*c*) Action to restore performance to the plan.

3. Cost consciousness. Many managers have a limited scope of action in the pursuit of profit. Indeed, only a few have responsibilities in the activities that actually generate income, for instance, the sales manager whose pricing decisions can increase sales revenue and thereby profit; most managers, however, are engaged solely in activities that incur costs, *e.g.* wages they pay to staff and operatives, materials they use and electricity they consume which are charges against company revenue and thereby constraints on profit. Nevertheless, they can play an equally important role as the income-earning manager in the generation of profit by minimising costs wherever possible. The following equation makes this self-evident:

$$\text{Profit} = \text{Total Revenue} - \text{Total Costs}$$

Thus a critical approach to costs by managers is vital for the efficient allocation of the resources under their control and thereby a direct contribution to the optimisation of profits. Certain principles are clear:

(*a*) Managers and staff must be educated to think in terms of cost control.

(*b*) A sound grasp of the nature of direct, indirect and semi-variable costs is important. Most managers appreciate the relationship between the employment of labour and use of materials and their costs. However, overheads may be considered erroneously to be solely fixed costs; the semi-variable aspect of certain overheads may therefore be overlooked so that heating, lights and machinery are left on unnecessarily. Similarly, stationery and consumables may be thoughtlessly over-ordered or their use uncontrolled so that additional yet avoidable costs are incurred.

(*c*) Managers should be encouraged to think of costs in terms of whether they are avoidable or not. A manager authorising or requesting authorisation of expenditure should compare the long-term costs with the anticipated short-term benefit. Costs may be distinguished as follows:

(*i*) Unavoidable costs (authorised).
(*ii*) Avoidable costs (requiring authorisation).

Unfortunately, expenditure once authorised has a tendency to become a permanent feature and unavoidable. Therefore managers must consider the long-term implication of authorisation and not simply the short-term benefits. Stories of staff carrying out costly and time-consuming but unnecessary work are legion (and in some cases factual), *e.g.* the preparing of monthly reports for senior management because a single instruction or authorisation of a request had been long forgotten.

(*d*) Managers should have a knowledge of certain cost concepts to give them greater breadth of vision and flexibility in planning and control. In particular the following concepts are important:

(*i*) Opportunity cost, which is the cost of the opportunity forgone when a decision is made.

(*ii*) Marginal costing and contribution analysis introduce flexibility into decision making.

4. Prerequisites for effective control. The following is a comprehensive list of principles for effective cost control:

(*a*) Cost centres must be clearly defined.

(*b*) Budgets must be established for each cost centre.

(*c*) Managers must appreciate the meaning and significance of direct cost and overheads and the relationship of each with output.

(*d*) All costs must be analysed in terms of the cost centres and charged to someone, *i.e.* every cost must be made the responsibility of somebody.

(*e*) Divergencies from the budget must be investigated. Divergencies from the budgeted costs are termed *variances*, hence the term *variance analysis* for this process of investigation. Clearly some divergencies are more important than others and since management's time is limited, it is essential that variance analysis is established on correct priorities so that important variances are dealt with first. However, where operations proceed to plan, management can pass over these areas of activities and instead concentrate on problem areas requiring their attention. This is known as "management by exception."

(*f*) Managers and staff must be critical. Ideally managers should be familiar with managerial economics for a knowledge of these principles and techniques may produce improvements in methods of operations and hence a better utilisation of resources.

(*g*) Managers must communicate effectively to seniors, subordinates and other managers in order to supply accurate information, issue clear instructions and generally secure the co-operation of others that is essential for the integration of departments.

5. Organisation chart.

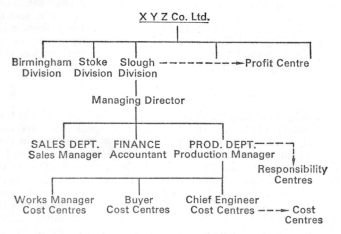

Fig. 38.—Organisation chart for XYZ Co. Ltd.

The above organisation chart is useful in defining the responsibilities of managers within an organisation, and illustrates the relationships between profit, responsibility and cost centres inherent in responsibility accounting. Here the Slough division of the XYZ Co. Ltd. is assumed to be autonomous with declared profit objectives which contribute with other divisions to the overall profitability of the XYZ organisation. At Slough the managing director is responsible for his division's performance.

One stage down the division's hierarchy of authority are the sales, finance and production managers with appropriate responsibilities to secure predetermined targets in each area. Each is allocated a number of accounts by the accountant which record the activities and enable the performance of each department to be assesssed.

Finally come the cost centres under the control of the chief engineer, buyer and works manager, all of whom are responsible to the production manager. The accountant and sales manager would have similar cost centres under their authority.

Thus the organisational chart is a useful way of defining the responsibilities of managers within a company, in that it identifies specific areas of responsibility of individual managers, clarifies areas where overlapping or doubt may exist and defines the hierarchy of authority structure. Only then, when responsibility is defined and is given to specific managers, can they be expected to control the costs incurred within their areas of responsibility.

BUDGETARY CONTROL

6. What are budgets? All managers are familiar with the term "budgetary control." Indeed most managers will have been directly involved in working to budgets at some stage in their career; the salesman working to the sales budget, the production manager to the production budget, the scientist to the research and development budget. However, the chances are that these managers, however expert in administering their own departmental or functional budgets, do not appreciate the interdependence and interlocking nature of individual budgets and are probably hazy about the purpose of the overall budget system, the nature of the many individual budgets and the responsibilities of their managers. Certainly the younger, newly-promoted manager, and the manager appointed from outside, face the problem of gaining a sound understanding of the budget system operated by the company in the shortest possible time.

The purpose of this chapter is to answer these problems rather than to concentrate on the technicalities involved in the day-to-day operations of specialist budgets.

7. The nature of budgetary control. Most shareholders, as owners of companies and senior managers, regard profit— whether defined as the maximum possible, or as a satisfactory level bearing in mind the risk inherent in the trade—as the most important corporate objective. However, profit does not exist as a right; it has to be created. Occasionally companies are lucky enough to receive windfall profits because of the vagaries of supply and demand in the market, but these tend to be unpredictable and therefore ignored by managers who prefer a more guaranteed and systematic approach to the creation of profits.

In other words, profits are planned, and in turn, integrated plans are drawn up for every part of the firm's operations which, if controlled, contribute to the overall planned profit. The firm is in fact an integrated system of parts, *e.g.* production department, purchasing department, stores and personnel, and decisions at every stage or by any part of the system create a ripple of effects throughout the system and an impact on profits. Some parts have different requirements and purposes. Indeed, they may conflict with others (*e.g.* sales and production where the former requires instant reaction to market changes while the latter favours stability of throughput), and it is a prerequisite of an integrated budgetary system that it reconciles such differences, and balances all parts within the system to achieve a complete, viable system.

8. Budget defined. The budget has been defined as:

"A financial and/or quantitative statement prepared prior to a defined period of time, of the policy to be pursued during that period for the purpose of attaining a given objective."

W. W. Bigg, *Cost Accounts*, Macdonald & Evans Ltd., ninth edition, 1972.

9. The budget period. This is a period selected by management for the preparation and employment of the budget. Obviously the period will be selected to suit the company or the industry. For example, a company in a fast-changing environment such as the fashion dress trade will naturally choose a short period; but a ship-building company may select eighteen months or two years because of the lengthy production periods.

However, subsidiary budgets should be broken down into shorter periods for management information purposes. Thus credit or cash budgets should be monthly or even more frequent. The budgeted profit and loss is often monthly or quarterly.

10. Explanation of the budget system. Figure 39 at first glance appears rather formidable. However, it is highly recommended that the reader analyses the diagram in conjunction with the explanatory notes that follow in order to secure a

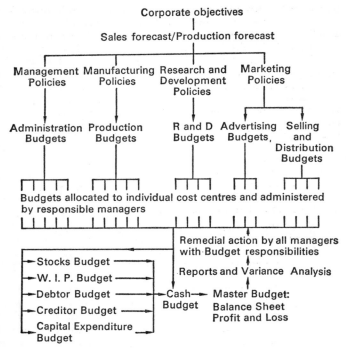

Fig. 39.—Overview of a total budget system.

sound understanding of the procedures and relationships contained in a comprehensive budget system. Clearly one diagram cannot describe every possible budget system since these vary from one company to the next depending on the nature of the business, but it does, however, describe the general budget pattern.

(a) *Corporate objectives*. This is the first step in developing a budgetary system, for precise goals are necessary to give management direction.

(b) *The sales forecast/production forecast*. The next most important step is the sales or production forecast:

(i) *The sales forecast* will take priority in management's

time and efforts if the company is newly established or is an existing company launching a new product. Clearly it must know in advance what it can reasonably expect to sell in physical and value terms. Market research and the opinions of salesmen and managers form the basis of the sales forecast.

(*ii*) *The production forecast* is more important when market demand is assured. Then the problem is one of producing sufficient goods to meet the demand, so calculations must be made of the output that management can reasonably expect from the employment of labour and equipment.

In a sense the capacity of the company becomes its sales forecast.

(*c*) *Policies.* The next step is to formulate policies to give functional managers direction of efforts and to set the pace of operations. Furthermore they must be integrated to direct the organisation towards the attainment of the sales/production forecast within the required time span.

(*i*) *Management policies.* These cover such areas as selection of personnel who possess the talents and experience needed throughout the organisation and the organisation of the general offices for the efficient operation of the administration function.

(*ii*) *Manufacturing policies* deal with plant layout, selection of tools and equipment and production systems.

(*iii*) *Research and development policies* deal with selection of projects and the relative priority between basic research and the development of commercial opportunities.

(*iv*) *Marketing policies.* These are closely related to the sales plan and relate to methods and amounts of advertising, the number of salesmen and their form of remuneration, etc.

(*d*) *Functional budgets.* Functional policies are formulated into plans (called budgets) for management, manufacturing, research and development and marketing which establish individual targets for each in terms of performance and costs. The respective managers are responsible for the implementation of their plan and seeing that operations proceed to plan.

(*e*) *Cost centre budgets.* Each functional budget is then subdivided into its major elements. Ideally a separate budget is established at points where costs are incurred on the grounds that expenses may be recorded and controlled directly and more efficiently. To take one example, the production budget will reflect the costs incurred by the press shop, machine shops 1 and 2, etc., and the assembly room, etc. in the employment of labour, use of materials and power. Each cost centre, whether location or operation, will have its own budget for which the appropriate managers and supervisors are responsible.

11. The capital budgets. Next, the various capital budgets are established on the basis of the relationship between anticipated revenue and expenditure. Furthermore, asset and liability values and profit figures are found by analysis of the various budgets, which enables the accountant to prepare a budgeted Balance Sheet and Profit and Loss Account. These final accounts summarise the anticipated profit and the consequences of trade on the company's assets and liabilities. However, the relationship between assets and liabilities and the resulting capital structure must not be fortuitous; the accountant must ensure throughout that the company's financial position remains sound. In particular, the credit that the company expects to give and take must be carefully balanced, for to give excessive credit could cause liquidity problems and the ability of the organisation to meet its short-term obligations and indeed its ability to survive.

The various capital budgets are as follows:

(*a*) *Stocks and work in progress.* These stock figures are arrived at by comparison of the sales and production budgets and after consideration of anticipated changes in activities, the relative costs of holding high stock levels and having money tied up and the benefits of bulk buying, etc.

(*b*) *Credit and debtor budgets.* These credit values are arrived at after examination of the sales and purchase budgets and the need for a satisfactory level of liquid funds.

(*c*) *Capital expenditure budget.* This consists of anticipated expenditure on fixed assets and is arrived at after examination of existing production facilities in relation to the level of production required by the sales budget. If present facilities are inadequate, then expenditure may be proposed for new plant and equipment or additional factory accommodation. Similarly, worn-out assets may need replacing.

(*d*) *Cash budget.* This budget lies at the centre of the budget system for it summarises all monetary receipts and payments recorded in all other budgets.

The value of cash receipts are anticipated by reference to the following factors:

(*i*) The level of cash sales from the sales budget.

(*ii*) The average collection period of debts due on the value of credit sales from the debtors' budget.

(*iii*) Other income, say, rents on accommodation sub-let.

The value of cash payments are calculated by reference to the following:

(*i*) Anticipated wages and salaries from the appropriate budget centres.

(*ii*) Expected purchases of raw materials from the materials budget.

(*iii*) Anticipated payments to creditors on the value of credit purchases considering the terms of credit contained in the contracts or established by trade custom.

(*iv*) Anticipated purchases of new assets from the capital expenditure budget.

12. The master budget. All the foregoing budgets are summarised to produce the master budget. Here, all proposed financial transactions are recorded and analysed to provide top management with an overall picture of what is expected at the end of the period under consideration. Furthermore, it frequently contains accounting ratios to test the anticipated liquidity, profitability, turnover of assets and profit margins. Areas of unsatisfactory performance can be investigated, remedial action taken and the appropriate budgets reworked.

13. Who supplies the forecasts? The budget as a planning device can only be as good as the forecasts on which it is based, so that the time and effort devoted at the outset to forecasting and appraising company resources can pay dividends in the long run. Furthermore, this preliminary work, although expensive, can be carried out effectively and the quality and reliability of information improved if the right people are involved. Obviously, the most suitably qualified people to advise on the setting of realistic forecasts are those most experienced or who are engaged in the day-to-day management in the particular field or activity. This is especially true if they operate a budget since their forecast may be based on the preceding budget suitably amended in the light of their experience and current objectives. The following example indicates which managers generally supply forecasts: naturally they are tentative at this early stage and may be amended several times before the budgets dove-tail into an integrated system.

Budget	Manager who advises on standard	Probable areas of advice
Sales	Sales manager	Selling price and volume costs
Production	Works manager	Output in units and value
Marketing	Sales or marketing manager	Advertising costs
Administration	Admin. manager or accountant	Salaries, rent, rates, legal fees etc.
Materials	Purchasing manager	Costs
Cash	Accountant	Based on information
Capital expenditure	Accountant	supplied in individual
Master budget	Accountant	budgets

Fig. 40.—Establishment of standards for the budget.

14. Limiting factors. In the formulation stage of the budgets, management may discover a limiting or governing factor that prevents the organisation from achieving the desired performance. For instance, there may be a serious shortage of materials which limits productive capacity so that the sales potential cannot be realised; or it may be that demand for the product is less than productive capacity. Quite obviously, serious consideration must be given to any limiting factors and remedies found by way of substitute materials or production methods or new markets and the budgets adjusted accordingly. Marginal analysis is helpful in this respect (*see* XI).

Finally, the master budget is approved and adopted by senior management and the decision taken to adopt the overall budget.

15. Control. Once operations start, close attention must be paid to actual performance and budgeted performance by managers and supervisors responsible for the individual budgets. Significant differences or *variances* should be investigated and remedial action taken.

This concludes the brief explanation of the inter-relationships of the various budgets described in the system in Figure 39. In summary then, the budget perhaps mistakenly regarded by some managers as a device for limiting expenditure is firmly established as a management technique designed to secure the most efficient use of the company's resources. It is essentially a detailed plan in quantitative and monetary terms for a specified period that provides for continuous monitoring and reviewing of performance against the established standards.

16. Advantages of a budget system. The advantages that may result from a budgetary control system may be listed as:

(a) The budget can usefully serve as a means of communication between top management and subordinate staff, and could make seniors more appreciative of subordinates' roles and problems.

(b) *Them and us* attitudes may lessen as each manager sees his own role in relation to the whole organisation.

(c) It can produce economies in management through the process of management by exception where managers focus their attention only where variances occur between performance and targets.

(d) It recognises the need for, and encourages delegation of responsibility, and participation by staff. Consequently, motivation and co-operation may be improved.

(e) Management can decentralise responsibility yet still through the budget maintain a central control over costs and performance.

17. Difficulties. However, the reader–manager may well know from personal experience that budgetary control systems are not without problems. Difficulties can arise in formulating the budget and in controlling to plan:

(a) The problem of setting realistic targets, for if the level is set too high and is unattainable, then morale will suffer, and if too low then inefficiency results.

(b) The budget can become an end in itself, and self-perpetuating without regular review and evaluation.

(c) It can be used as a pressure device to promote the ends of sectional interests.

(d) The budget may come to be regarded as an end in

itself if the objectives of the budgetary system are not emphasised and sold to the staff who must implement it.

(e) It can become cumbersome and less productive in time, and thereby hide inefficiency.

EXAMPLES OF BUDGETARY DOCUMENTS

18. Choice of examples. The following examples of specific budgets and documents associated with a budgetary control system have been selected for the following reasons.

(a) To provide a back-up for and, in part, to quantify the description of the budgetary system outlined in the introduction.

(b) To provide the reader with an idea of the style and content of typical budget statements.

(c) To illustrate how overheads are allocated among cost centres.

(d) To distinguish between fixed and variable budgets.

(e) To illustrate the typical form of the master budget and the cash budget, the two most important parts of the system.

19. Administration budget. This budget deals with all the costs of management and the general offices and normally covers a budget period of one year, as can be seen in Fig. 41.

Item		Total
Directors' fees (fixed cost)		£10,000
Legal fees	"	2,000
Rates	"	1,000
Rent	"	2,000
Management salaries	"	15,000
Telephone (semi-variable costs)		500
Travel	"	1,000
Stationery	"	300
Depreciation	"	500
Clerical salaries	"	10,000
		£42,300

Fig. 41.—Administration budget to year end 1975.

These costs are typical of the administration function, but they are not an exhaustive list. Moreover, they all relate to one function and do not include similar expenses incurred in other functions or departments, *e.g.* the salaries of office workers within the purchasing, selling, production areas, etc.

This budget is probably one of the easiest to establish since many of the costs are fixed for the year and the remainder possess fixed cost characteristics, *i.e.* they are semi-variable.

20. Sales overhead budget. This budget differs from the previous example in that it is made up of certain overhead costs that cannot be traced directly to this specific cost centre, but which are nevertheless apportioned or charged by some predetermined formula for benefits received. The accountant and sales manager are the probable sources of such information.

Variable overheads		*i*		*ii*	*iv*	*v*
Salesmen commissions	(2%)	£ 6,000	6,400	6,800	7,200	7,600
Carriage outwards	(5%)	15,000	16,000	17,000	18,000	19,000
		£21,000	22,400	23,800	25,200	26,600
Fixed overheads						
Office salaries		3,000	3,000	3,000	3,000	3,000
Office expenses		2,000	2,000	2,000	2,000	2,000
Salesmen salaries		4,000	4,000	4,000	4,000	4,000
Total overheads		£ 30,000	31,400	32,800	34,200	35,600
Sales anticipated		£300,000	320,000	340,000	360,000	380,000
Sales percentage		88%	94%	100%	105%	112%

Fig. 42.—Sales overheads budget for month ending 31.12.74.

The budget shows that if sales are £300,000 (Column *i*), then the direct costs of salesmen commissions and carriage outwards amount to £21,000. Adding on fixed overheads then total overheads amount to £30,000.

21. Flexible budgets. The above example also serves to illustrate a *flexible* budget. Here a range of sales values is estimated for January from £300,000 to £380,000. If a sales value of £340,000 is most likely and is regarded as the norm of 100 per cent, then we have a percentage range of sales from 88 to 112 per cent. Variable costs are then calculated for every sales value.

The purpose is that sales are unlikely to match exactly the

anticipated level of £340,000; there may be production difficulties, shortages of materials or new products by competitors
so that sales are only 88 per cent of those expected. However,
this flexible budget contains variable and fixed costs for this
level of activity, which facilitates a comparison of the actual
sales overhead costs with the budgeted costs.

On the other hand, the master budget (*see* below) is an
example of a *fixed* budget.

22. Master budget. The master budget may take the following forms:

(*a*) A budgeted Profit and Loss A/C and Balance Sheet.
(*b*) A summary of the principal budgets. It frequently
includes a break-even graph.

	Budget		Actual		Remarks
(*i*) Sales	* *		* *		
Manufacturing costs	* *		* *		
Factory labour	* *		* *		
Factory materials	* *		* *		
Factory overheads	* *		* *		
+ opening stocks	* *		* *		
− closing stocks	* *		* *		
(*ii*) Factory cost of goods sold	* *	* *	* *	* *	
(*iii*) GROSS PROFIT (*i*) − (*ii*)		* *		* *	
(*iv*) Expenses					
Administration	* *		* *		
Selling and distribution	* *	* *	* *	* *	
NET PROFIT (*iii*) − (*iv*)		* *		* *	
(*v*) Capital employed	* *		* *		
Ratios					
(*vi*) Return on capital employed	* *		* *		
(*vii*) Return on equity	* *		* *		
(*viii*) Current ratio	* *		* *		
(*ix*) Quick ratio	* *		* *		
(*x*) Asset turnover	* *		* *		

Fig. 43.—Master budget for year ending 31.12.75.

23. Cash budget. All budgets concerned with monetary transactions are related to the cash budget. By forecasting receipts and incorporating all anticipated demands on the company's cash resources, management can make realistic policy decisions, ensure that cash is available to finance production to meet the anticipated sales, finance capital expenditures and give prompt attention to the problems of cash shortfall or surpluses.

	Jan.	Feb.	Mar.
Cash sales	* *	* *	* *
Receipts from debtors	* *	* *	* *
(*i*) *Total cash receipts*	* *	* *	* *
Wages	* *	* *	* *
Purchases	* *	* *	* *
Expenses	* *	* *	* *
New plant	* *	* *	* *
(*ii*) *Total cash payments*	* *	* *	* *
(*iii*) Net change in cash (*i*) − (*ii*)	* *	* *	* *
(*iv*) Cash balance b/f	* *	* *	* *
(*v*) Cash in hand (*iii*) + (*iv*)	* *	* *	* *

FIG. 44.—Cash budget for year ending 31.12.74.

24. Working capital forecast. The following calculation is a simple yet effective way of forecasting the short-term working capital requirements. It is suitable for small companies and is generally used in the construction industry. Let us assume that the company, a building firm, allocates general overheads on the basis of 50 per cent of operatives' wages, and that materials are estimated to be 200 per cent of operatives' wages. The company takes six weeks' credit from trade merchants for materials and is paid after six weeks by the client (debtor) for the value of work executed during the period.

In this example the company employing a hundred operatives requires £45,000 working capital to finance operations. Fortunately the trade merchants finance materials but it is clear that any delay in payment by the debtor means that additional funds must be found to pay for these materials as well as extra wages and overhead expenses.

Data:
(*i*)	Number of operatives	100 men
(*ii*)	Credit period granted to customers	6 weeks
(*iii*)	Average operatives' wage	£50 per week
(*iv*)	Cost of materials 200% × (*iii*)	£100 per week
(*v*)	Credit period granted by company to client	6 weeks

Calculations of working capital
(*vi*)	Wages to be financed (*ii*) × (*iii*)	£300
(*vii*)	General overheads financed (*vi*) × 50%	150
(*viii*)	Materials (*iv*) × ((*ii*) − (*v*))	—

Total working capital/operative   £450

Total working capital for 100 operatives £45,000

Fig. 45.—Calculation of working capital required.

ADMINISTRATION OF THE BUDGET

25. The budget committee. It is an accepted rule that to secure the successful implementation and working of a budgetary control system, managers who are responsible for the carrying out of budgets must be consulted and involved at the formulation stage. Their active co-operation is often established through the budget committee which has the following functions:

(*a*) Compilation of the outline budget programme.
(*b*) Examination and solution of problems to secure co-ordination and amendment of budget for approval by top management.
(*c*) Ensuring that the system is implemented.
(*d*) Ensuring that the system is controlled.

26. The budget officer. In larger organisations, a budget officer is appointed to carry out the policy decisions of the budget committee and the day-to-day work involved in operating the budget system. In particular, his functions are to:

(*a*) Serve as secretary to the budget committee.
(*b*) Communicate the committee's instructions.
(*c*) Assemble information for the committee's consideration.

(*d*) Co-ordinate the preparation of individual budgets.
(*e*) Prepare the master budget.
(*f*) Analyse and report on budget performance to the committee and appropriate managers.

27. The budget manual. Larger companies publish a manual on their budget system. It may contain:

(*a*) Objectives of the system.
(*b*) Statement of responsibilities of budget managers.
(*c*) The budget period.
(*d*) Timetable for preparation and amendments of budgets.
(*e*) Procedures to be followed.
(*f*) Specimens of budget documents.

The purpose is to achieve an efficient budgetary control system by assigning responsibility in a clear manner, standardising procedures and motivating personnel through their participation and the formal publication of company policy.

CONTROLLING TO PLAN

28. The need for information. At this stage, it is important to restate the purpose of the budgetary control system . . . a financial system that summarises corporate plans, compares actual and planned performance, and highlights areas for remedial actions for the purpose of attaining a given objective. Clearly control is a vital element and to be effective, information on current performance must be immediately available to responsible managers who exercise control. This information is usually supplied by the management accountant in the form of reports, operating statements and graphs.

29. Budget reports. There is a two-way flow of information between the cost centre manager and the management accountant or budget officer. The former is responsible for authorising payments, and copies of all initialled documents are remitted to the accountant who records and analyses costs for each centre. Periodically the accountant sends a report telling the budget manager how his cost centre has performed to date. Ideally the budget report should:

(a) Show deviations of actual performance from that planned (i.e. variances, see **30**).
(b) Be available quickly so that action can be taken without delay.
(c) Be in a standard form to facilitate comprehension.

Product	Month of February *This period*											
	Budgeted			Actual				Budgeted		Actual		
	Units	Price	£	Units	Price	£	Variance	Units	£	Units	£	Variance
X	1,000	£3	3,000	500	£2	1,000	£2,000	2,000	6,000	1,500	4,000	£2,000
Y	2,000	£2	4,000	2,000	£2	4,000	—	4,000	8,000	4,000	8,000	—
Z	3,000	£1	3,000	2,000	£1	2,000	£1,000	6,000	6,000	5,000	5,000	£1,000
Total	6,000		10,000	4,500		7,000		12,000	20,000	10,500	17,000	£3,000

Remarks on variances:

i Product	ii Variance	iii Cause	iv Possible action
X	Units and price are less than expected. Units 500 less; price £1 less. Sales value £2,000 less than budget.	Fall in demand: £1 price cut by the company.	Increase in advertising? Sales campaign to increase demand?
Y	Nil	—	—
Z	Units are less than expected, i.e. by 1,000 units. Sales value £1,000 less than budget.	Delay in dispatch.	Increase overtime? Increase staff in dispatch?

NOTE: The above variances for February explain why budgeted and actual sales figures to date differ. Columns iii and iv have been inserted to give the reader an idea of possible analysis and courses of action available to management.

FIG. 46.—Sales report (or Sales operating statement).

30. Variances. A variance is the difference between planned and actual performance. At the operating level it is expressed in terms of quantities but for senior management purposes is converted into monetary terms. Thus it becomes:

    (a) The difference between planned and actual costs, or
    (b) the difference between planned and actual revenue, or
    (c) the difference between planned and actual profit.

Where performance is better than budget the variance is termed *favourable*; where worse it is *adverse*.

31. Purpose of budget reports or variance statements. These are essentially means by which senior management and budget managers can measure performance.

    (a) They enable senior management to:

        (i) measure overall performance and review future policy;
        (ii) measure budget managers' performance and review possible actions;
        (iii) measure the degree to which variances are outside the control of these managers and review possible actions.

    (b) They enable budget managers to:

        (i) measure their success in carrying out their responsibilities and review future actions;
        (ii) measure the extent to which variances are outside their control.

32. Controllable and uncontrollable costs. It is a basic tenet of budgetary control that managers should be responsible for the costs they control. Thus in the budget report, controllable and uncontrollable variances are distinguished. For instance, this would show the materials budget manager that labour (especially if overtime is worked) and office stationery costs are controllable, and that if these variances are adverse, remedial action on his part is required. Additionally, it might state adverse variances for raw materials, rent and rates which are uncontrollable by this manager since they are set by, say, the commodity market and the landlord, council, or accountant respectively.

33. The need for standards of performance. So far no mention has been made of setting standards of performance and costs at the planning stage. Yet this is vital if the organisation is to be planned and controlled effectively. Positive efforts must be made at the outset to lay down standards that, if achieved, result in a desired level of efficiency. Obviously the standards must not be set too high nor too low nor simply based on previous years' figures.

In summary, a budgetary control system without standards is meaningless and a waste of time and expense, for if based on too high standards it may be self-defeating, and if too low it may encourage inefficiency.

34. Standard costs. Standard or planned costs are often introduced into budgetary control systems. This is a realistic assessment of the expected cost of an operation based on an efficient level of activity. Similarly standard revenue, standard output and profit figures are established as planned targets. Its introduction enables managers to compare actual with planned performance by means of variances right down to the small items of detail that make up the budget. For example, items of expenditure on material, labour, fixed and variable overheads incurred in the production of a component at, say, the Engineering Shop cost centre, can be controlled by analysis of variances.

PROGRESS TEST 10

1. Define the following:
   (a) management by exception;
   (b) organisation chart;
   (c) profit centres;
   (d) responsibility centres. (1–5)

2. Define a budget and explain a typical budgetary control system. (6–17)

3. What are the advantages of a flexible budget? (20–21)

4. "Activities must be controlled to plan and remedial action taken without delay." Discuss. (28–34)

CHAPTER XI

PLANNING FOR PROFIT

MARGINAL COSTING

1. Marginal costs. Marginal cost is the additional cost of producing one extra unit, *i.e.* the cost of the marginal unit. Thus if 100 units are produced for a total cost of £250 and 101 units for £252, then the marginal cost is £2. In fact, marginal cost is the same as variable cost which can be seen from the following:

fixed costs + variable costs = total costs
£50 + £200   = £250 (for 100 units)
£50 + £202   = £252 (for 101 units)

Clearly the additional cost is £2 (£252 — £250) and results directly from the extra wages and material costs involved in producing the extra unit (since fixed costs are constant).

2. Contribution. Contribution is the difference between selling price and marginal (variable) cost:

contribution = selling price — marginal cost

But contribution to what? To answer this we must consider the special treatment of fixed costs in marginal costing. They are not apportioned to units of output as in full cost pricing, but are set aside and eventually covered by a fund of contributions realised by the sale of individual units of output. Clearly, if total contributions exceed fixed costs then profits are made:

Product A
Sales revenue — marginal costs = contribution
Product B
Sales revenue — marginal costs = contribution
Product C, etc.
Sales revenue — marginal costs = contribution

Total contributions towards

fixed costs and profit

165

3. Importance of marginal costing. Marginal costing and contribution analysis are extremely useful tools for management in decision making and cost control. Marginal costing is particularly important in short-term analysis of management problems; its flexibility and the scope for its application in the areas of pricing, costing and resource allocation are valid reasons for mastering the concept.

4. Examples of areas where it may be applied:

(*a*) Pricing.
(*b*) Allocation of scarce resources between competing uses.
(*c*) Make or buy analysis.
(*d*) Close-down decisions.
(*e*) Comparisons of production methods.

5. Pricing decisions. Marginal costing allows management greater flexibility in setting selling price than full cost pricing permits. In fact price may be set below total cost. For instance, if marginal (variable) costs are £20 per unit, fixed costs are £40,000, and anticipated sales 3,900 units at £30 each, then:

$$\text{At Fixed Cost} \quad + \text{Variable Cost}$$
$$\text{Total cost per unit} = £40,000 \div 3,900 + £20$$
$$= £30\text{·}25$$

This company tendering for an additional order of 300 units might base its price on full cost of £29·52:

$$\text{Total cost per unit} = £40,000 \div 4,200 + £20$$
$$= £9\text{·}52 + £20$$
$$= £29\text{·}52$$

However, using marginal pricing, a lower price is possible: a price of £27 might be low enough to secure the contract and yet provide an overall profit of £1,100.

Anticipated sales;			*Total contribution*
Selling price — Vble cost = contribution			£10 × 3,900 units
£30 — £20 = £10/unit			= £39,000
Sales:			£7 × 300 = £2,100
£27 — £20 = £7/unit			= £41,100—£40,000 overheads
			= profit £1,100

Contract: £39,000
                                    =   2,100
                                        ───────
                                         41,100
                                    —   40,000 overhead
                                        ───────
                                          1,100 profit

A further example of marginal pricing is found in the travel industry. Package tour operators who book hotels for the whole year earn sufficient revenue in the peak periods to cover fixed costs and to provide profit, but they offer off-season rates at marginal cost (the cost of travel, accommodation, food, etc.) which is preferable to closing down the hotels.

(*a*) Off-season rates of, say, £5 per week cover marginal costs and may make small contributions to profit.

(*b*) Overall profits are increased as long as peak bookings are maintained. However, if holidaymakers substitute the cheaper off-peak holidays for peak period holidays, fixed cost may not be covered.

(*c*) Hotel services are maintained and hotel staff retained.

Similarly, air-carriers offer cheaper charter rates based on marginal cost of transport which makes a contribution to the air-lines' overheads.

6. Allocation of scarce resources. Profitability depends on the optimum allocation of resources between competing uses. Thus if management is faced with a scarcity of a factor of production (termed a *limiting* or *key* factor), it must ensure that profits per unit of key factor are maximised. This is achieved by maximising contribution per unit of key factor since fixed costs remain constant in the short term.

EXAMPLE. Veneered Table Tops Limited manufactures coffee and telephone table tops for the furniture industry. Costing details are as follows:

	Coffee table tops		*Telephone table tops*	
Variable costs				
Wood 2 cu. ft. @ £3·00	£6·00	2·25 cu. ft. @ £3·00	£6·75
Labour 2 hours @ 75p	1·50	1½ hours @ 75p	1·12
Expenses 2 hours @ 50p	1·00	1½ hours @ 50p	·75
Total variable costs per unit	8·50		8·62
Contribution: Selling price	10·00		10·00
Less: Variable cost	8·50		8·62
	£1·50		£1·38

It should be noted that management must organise output to take into account the following circumstances:

(a) Staff holidays in August when labour hours will be the key or limiting factor acting as a constraint on production;
(b) a shortage of wood in September brought about by fire at the local wood stockist.

These problems can be solved by analysis of the contributions per unit of limiting factor:

$$(a) \text{ Contribution per unit of labour} = \frac{\text{contribution}}{\text{labour hours}}$$

(i) Contribution per unit of labour (coffee table)
$$= \frac{£1\cdot50}{2}$$
$$= 75\text{p}$$

(ii) Contribution per unit of labour (telephone table)
$$= \frac{£1\cdot38}{1\cdot5}$$
$$= 92\text{p}$$

$$(b) \text{ Contribution per unit of wood} = \frac{\text{contribution}}{\text{cubic feet of wood}}$$

(i) Contribution per unit of wood (coffee table)
$$= \frac{£1\cdot50}{2}$$
$$= 75\text{p}$$

(ii) Contribution per unit of wood (telephone table)
$$= \frac{£1\cdot38}{2\cdot25}$$
$$= 61\text{p}$$

Management can allocate the scarce resources most efficiently by concentrating on telephone tables in August and coffee tables in September, which thereby maximises contributions of the limiting factors of labour and wood respectively.

7. Make or buy analysis. Managers may occasionally be faced with the problem of whether to continue to make a product or to buy from an outside supplier. The decision obviously depends on the relative profitability which is measured by comparison of the purchase price and the marginal cost of production, since fixed costs exist in the short-term whether the goods are produced or not. Let us assume that the company producing two products X and Y, has limited machine capacity and that the comparative cost data is as follows:

	Product X	Product Y
Marginal (variable) costs	£5	£7
Purchase price	£7	£10
Difference	£2	£3
Machine times	45 mins.	25 mins.
Difference per machine hour	£2·66	£7·20

This shows that to produce products X and Y costs £2·66 and £7·20 per machine hour in excess of the price of buying from outside. Consequently, profits would be improved if product Y were purchased, and the machine capacity so released used for the production of X.

8. Close-down decision. Management may face the problem of temporarily closing down a department or factory which is making losses. On cost grounds there is a strong case for maintaining operations while sales revenue exceeds variable costs since a contribution is made towards fixed costs. To close down the department or factory would not avoid the fixed costs, so any contribution to fixed costs and which reduces the amount of the trading loss is preferred.

Figure 47 illustrates this point. Break-even occurs at a selling price of OP and output and sales of OQ, *i.e.* total revenue (price OP × quantity OQ = the area bounded by the points OPTQ) is equal to total cost (cost per unit OP × quantity OQ = OPTQ). Whenever selling price is below OP then total revenue is less than total cost so that losses are incurred.

If price is OP_1 then total revenue is OP_1VQ, total cost is OPTQ and the loss is P_1PTV which is equal to the fixed cost.

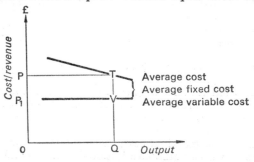

FIG. 47.—Break-even graph.

EXAMPLE

$$\text{Total cost} = \text{total variable cost} + \text{fixed cost}$$
$$\text{OPTQ} = \text{OP}_1\text{VQ} + \text{fixed cost}$$
$$\text{Fixed cost} = \text{total cost} - \text{total variable cost}$$
$$\text{Fixed cost} = \text{OPTQ} - \text{OP}_1\text{VQ}$$
$$= \text{P}_1\text{PTV}$$

It follows that:

(a) If selling price is below OP_1, fixed cost and part of variable costs are not covered. The firm on cost grounds should close down and minimise the size of the loss to the value of fixed costs.

(b) If price is above OP_1 but below OP, variable costs are covered and a contribution is made to fixed costs. Here losses are less than the value of fixed costs and are therefore minimised if the company continues to operate.

9. Non-cost considerations. Non-cost factors must be considered in arriving at a closure decision:

(a) Suspension of activities may adversely affect customer goodwill and loss of business in the future.

(b) The firm may get a bad reputation as an employer, which will cause difficulties in staff recruitment.

10. Comparisons of production methods. Management may have a choice between methods of production. For instance:

	Method 1		Method 2
Sales 1,000 units @ £20	£20,000		£20,000
Variable costs 1,000 units @ £10	£10,000	@ £14	£14,000
Contribution	£10,000		£6,000
Fixed costs per method	£7,000		£2,000
Contribution to factory overheads	£3,000		£4,000

Here Method 1 makes the larger contribution to fixed costs, but Method 2 secures a larger overall contribution to factory overheads and is preferable to Method 1.

11. Dangers of marginal costing. Marginal costing provides the manager with a valuable additional technique for decision-making. However, the manager is not advised to apply it unthinkingly: it may provide pitfalls for the unwary. The main dangers are:

(*a*) The manager might lose sight of the fact that in the longer term, prices must be sufficient to cover total costs.

(*b*) Its usefulness is limited where a manufacturer manufactures a standard product that sells in a single market. Clearly there is no possibility of price discrimination in this situation; to base price on variable cost would mean disaster.

(*c*) Customers could react unfavourably to a price policy based on marginal costs that continually changed because of movements in labour and material costs.

(*d*) Additional sales secured through marginal costing must be justified and not become an end in themselves. Thus if sales have to be diverted from profitable markets in order to meet contracts priced on a marginal basis, overall contributions are reduced.

PROGRESS TEST 11

1. Explain the following:
   (*a*) fixed cost;
   (*b*) variable cost;
   (*c*) marginal cost;
   (*d*) contribution. (1–3)
2. Illustrate four areas in which marginal costing can play a useful role. (3–10)
3. "Marginal costing has its shortcomings." Discuss. (11)

CHAPTER XII

BREAK-EVEN ANALYSIS

INTRODUCTION

1. The use of break-even. Break-even analysis simplifies the complex relationship between revenue cost and output by reducing it to visual form, and is strongly recommended to the reader–manager on the grounds that a sound grasp of how changes in output affect company revenue/costs—and thereby profits—is essential for successful management. Some managers acquire through experience an intuitive feel for the situation, but newer, less experienced men are advised to study break-even analysis and apply the technique to their own situation. Its versatility and potential is considerable and may well provide a fresh approach to old problems.

2. Definition of break-even. Break-even is defined as the level of activity where no profits are made or losses incurred. In other words, that level of operations where total costs equal total revenue.

3. Total cost: the economist's viewpoint. Total cost is the sum of all costs incurred in an operation so that if we classify costs under the headings of fixed and variable then we have the equation:

Total costs = fixed costs + variable costs

(*a*) Fixed costs are said to be *time based*. In other words, certain costs, *e.g.* rent and rates, interest on loans and management salaries are constant in the short-run, regardless of the level of activity: they remain the same whether output is zero or 100 per cent. However, these costs change in the long run; rent and rates will go up, the loan may be extinguished and management's salaries will increase at the annual review. Everything is uncertain and variable in the long-run except one certainty—for as Lord Keynes, the eminent economist said "In the long run we are all dead!"

(b) Variable costs by definition vary with the level of activity, *e.g.* wages of direct labour, costs of materials and power although they may not vary directly. In fact at low levels of activity, variable costs rise, as additional workers are taken on, less steeply than output because of the operation of the law of increasing returns; eventually at high levels of operations the law of diminishing returns may cause variable costs to rise faster than output.

Thus in the short-run, the continuous total cost curve for a typical industrial organisation make-up of fixed costs and variable costs will appear as in Fig. 48.

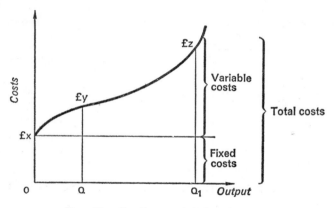

FIG. 48.—Continuous total cost curve.

When output is OQ, total cost is £y;
FC = £x, VC = £y − £x.
When output is OQ₁, total cost is £z;
FC = £x, VC = £z − £x.

From Fig. 48 we conclude that the economist is interested in the behaviour of fixed and variable costs over the entire range of the company's activities in the short run, *i.e.* from an output of a single unit to full capacity.

4. Total revenue: the economist's viewpoint. Economic theory, supported by market research, states that all companies, whether in a competitive market or in a monopolistic situation, are subject to a law of downward sloping demand (*see* Fig. 49). This means that they are incapable of supplying an infinite quantity of their goods at a fixed price. Eventually, at a high sales volume, suppliers encounter resistance on the part of the customer and reactions by competitors which force them to reduce price. Naturally this has a direct effect on sales revenue; it will decline relative to sales volume when price cuts are made and may fall in absolute terms if the price cuts are substantial.

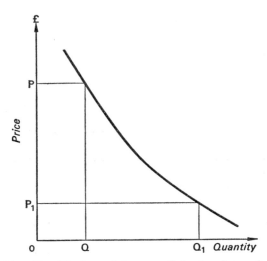

Fig. 49.—The law of downward sloping demand.

(*i*) High price OP — small amount demanded OQ.
(*ii*) Low price OP$_1$ — large amount demanded OQ$_1$.

Fig. 50 contains a typical total revenue curve that is based on a demand curve that slopes downwards to the right as in Fig. 49. The total cost curve from Fig. 48 is superimposed for comparison.

5. Break-even graph and company objectives. Fig. 50 illustrates the economist's attitudes to total costs and total revenue. He considers the effect on each of a continuous increase in

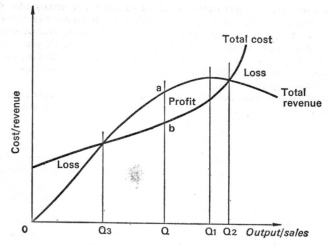

FIG. 50.—Break-even graph.

output and sales from zero to full capacity, and thereby builds up a complete picture of the cost/revenue relationship which we may use for analysis of company objectives. Two break-even levels of output/sales are shown, OQ_3 and OQ_2. If activity is below OQ_3, total costs exceed total revenue so that losses are incurred in the range from O to Q_3. Between OQ_3 and OQ_2 revenue exceeds costs, a profitable range and beyond OQ_2 costs are greater than revenue so that losses are made.

Four frequently quoted objectives of companies are:

(a) Maximisation of profits.
(b) Maximisation of sales volume.
(c) Maximisation of sales revenue.
(d) A satisfactory level of profitability.

At this stage we can deal with (a), (b) and (c); (d) is more complicated and is dealt with later in the chapter.

6. Maximisation of profits. This is achieved at a level of activity when, using the economist's terminology, marginal cost is equal to marginal revenue. In other words, if at a lower level of activity the extra revenue exceeds the extra cost of producing and selling one more unit, then total profits can be improved by producing and selling this extra unit. If, however, the extra cost exceeds the extra revenue of an incremental unit of output, less total profit will be made. The intermediate position where marginal cost and revenue are equal secures maximum profits.

The reader who has no training in economics will certainly appreciate this concept of profit maximisation if instead of marginal analysis we use the equation:

$$\text{Profit} = \text{total sales revenue} - \text{total costs}$$

Clearly it is a condition, if profits are to be maximised, that total sales revenue must exceed total costs by the greatest possible amount. In Fig. 50 this occurs at a level of output/sales of OQ; a b is the longest possible vertical line between the total revenue and total cost curves.

In summary, the break-even graph indicates the level of activity required to meet the objective of maximisation of profits. This occurs at that level of output/sales where:

(a) Marginal cost equals marginal revenue.

(b) The slope of the total revenue curve equals the slope of the total cost curve.

(c) The vertical difference between these curves is maximised.

7. Maximisation of sales volume. The firm may be motivated to maximise the number of units sold or the money value of their sales for reasons of prestige or market domination. Furthermore, energies and resources directed into building up the size of the organisation may serve the interests of managers whose power, career development and salaries are related to the size of the organisation.

The level of output that satisfies the sales/volume–maximisers requirement is OQ_2 in Fig. 50. In fact the company breaks even, for examination of the Figure shows that at this level of activity total revenue is equal to total cost.

Sales/output activity beyond OQ_2 means that losses are incurred, since total costs exceed total revenue, and although such activity satisfies the assumed goal it is uneconomic and cannot be sustained indefinitely. Indeed it is doubtful whether the break-even sales/output level of OQ_2 is no more than a very short-run equilibrium, for although no losses are incurred, neither are profits made. Obviously not a healthy situation for survival.

8. Maximisation of sales revenue. Money value of sales are maximised at a level of activity where the total revenue curve is at its highest point, *i.e.* OQ_1. In the economists' terminology, where the marginal revenue is zero.

9. Break-even: the accountant's viewpoint. We have considered briefly the attitude of the economist to break-even; how he analyses the behaviour of continuous total costs and revenue over the company's entire output/sales range. However, the accountant is directly concerned with supplying management with past and future information of costs and revenue for a limited range of activities. Furthermore, since he is primarily interested in the operational range, and although he may appreciate the underlying assumptions and behaviour of costs and revenue at very low and high levels of activities, he considers them to be irrelevant to the immediate management decisions.

Consequently, the accountant uses break-even analysis, suitably modified, in the following ways:

(*a*) Total costs are represented by a straight line which tends to approximate to the actual values over the narrow production range.

(*b*) Total revenue is represented by a straight line, on the assumption that moderate percentage increases in sales may be achieved without price cutting.

(*c*) These curves may be extended outside the narrow operational range and may illustrate the approximate cost/revenue/volume relationship as long as the limitations are remembered, *i.e.* revenue and costs are in fact non-linear over the entire range of activities.

It should be noted that in Fig. 51:

(*a*) Assumed normal operational range of output is $Q - Q_2$.

(*b*) Profit at an output of OQ_2 is £a, b.

(*c*) The graph shows that if output could be increased to OQ_3 then profit could be increased to £c, d.

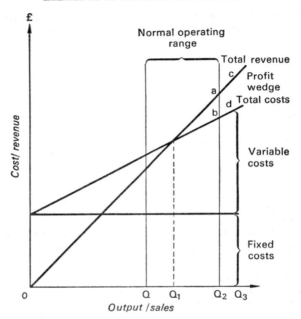

FIG. 51.—Straight line break-even graph.

(d) Any level of output beyond OQ_1 (the break-even) is profitable.

(e) It shows the revenue/cost relationship at different levels of output, and not that the company initially makes losses and profits later in the year. Time is ignored and does not appear on the horizontal axis.

10. Calculation of break-even. The break-even level of activity can be calculated by formulae as a check on the accuracy of the graph. The formulae are as follows:

(a) Break-even sales revenue $= \dfrac{\text{fixed cost}}{1 - \dfrac{\text{variable cost}}{\text{selling price}}}$

(b) Break-even sales volume $= \dfrac{\text{fixed cost}}{\text{selling price} - \text{variable cost}}$

11. Limitations of straightline break-even. Managers who construct or read break-even charts should always bear in mind the following limitations:

(*a*) In practice the cost/volume relationship is not necessarily linear.

(*b*) In practice the revenue/volume relationship is not necessarily linear. In other words it is dangerous to extrapolate the curves outside the normal range of activity. To resist this temptation, managers should be made aware of the economist's analysis on the behaviour of cost, revenue and volume and the relationship between each.

(*c*) Profits are not necessarily maximised at maximum output (OQ_3 in Fig. 51), since in practice:

(*i*) The revenue curve may be lower than shown because of discounts and price cuts to achieve this high level of sales.

(*ii*) The cost curve may be higher than shown because of disproportionate increases in variable costs, *e.g.* overtime, shift work payments to achieve this high output.

(*d*) It is a static illustration of a dynamic situation and therefore must be updated regularly.

(*e*) It assumes that sales and output are in balance, *i.e.* all that is produced is sold within the same time period.

(*f*) Fixed costs may in fact change. For example, to obtain high levels of output, additional machines or staff may be taken on. Thus the fixed cost curve is not perfectly horizontal but is *stepped* (*see* Fig. 52); the total cost curve is similarly stepped.

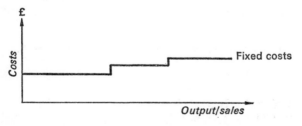

FIG. 52.—Stepped fixed costs.

TYPES OF BREAK-EVEN GRAPHS

12. Contribution break-even graph. Contribution is simply the difference between selling price and variable costs. Thus if a product sells for £6·00 and the variable costs, consisting of direct wages, materials and other direct expenses, amount to £3·00, the contribution is £3·00.

Contribution = selling price — variable costs
£3·00   =   £6·00   —   £3·00

This £3·00, along with other contributions, goes into a fund which is used to meet the fixed costs and to provide a profit. For example, if fixed costs amount to £10,000, and 7,000 units are sold, then:

Total contribution — fixed cost = profit
£3·00 × 7,000   — £10,000   = £11,000

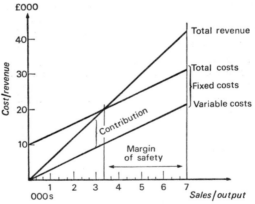

Fig. 53.—Contribution break-even for Product A.

The contribution break-even is graphed in the following steps:

(*a*) Draw in the variable cost curve.

(*b*) Add fixed costs to the variable cost curve. This line represents total costs (TC = FC + VC).

(*c*) Draw in the sales revenue line.

13. Analysis of contribution break-even graph.

(a) Examination of the graph shows that break-even is 3,333 units and with a sales value of £20,000. The accuracy of the graph is checked by calculation.

$$(i) \text{ Break-even} = \frac{\text{fixed cost}}{1 - \dfrac{\text{variable cost}}{\text{selling price}}}$$

$$= \frac{£10,000}{1 - \dfrac{3}{6}}$$

$$= £20,000$$

$$(ii) \text{ Break-even} \atop \text{(sales volume)} = \frac{\text{fixed cost}}{\text{selling price} - \text{variable cost}}$$

$$= \frac{£10,000}{£6 - £3}$$

$$= 3,333 \text{ units}$$

(b) Furthermore, the contribution towards fixed costs can be read off for a given level of activity. Thus the contribution measured by the vertical distance between the variable cost line and the revenue line is:

(i) £6,000 at output and sales of 2,000 units, and
(ii) £15,000 at output and sales of 5,000 units, etc.

14. Profit/volume (P/V) ratio.
This ratio, more accurately described as the contribution/sales ratio, measures contribution as a percentage of sales value.

$$P/V = \frac{\text{contribution}}{\text{selling price}} \times 100$$

$$= \frac{\text{selling price} - \text{variable cost}}{\text{selling price}} \times 100$$

Table XII shows applications of the P/V ratio. Applying the formula, the P/V ratio for product A is 50 per cent $\left(\dfrac{£10 - £5 \times 100}{£10} \right)$ and 62 and 71 per cent for B and C respectively. Since contribution and sales are in direct proportion, total contributions can be calculated (P/V × sales value) for a given amount of sales value. Clearly product C is preferred to A and B on the grounds that it makes the highest unit contribution to overheads and profits, and therefore management

TABLE XII.—APPLICATIONS OF THE P/V RATIO.

Product	Selling price	Variable cost	Contribution	P/V	Sales value	Total contribution
A	£10	£5	£5	50%	£80,000	£40,000
B	£8	£3	£5	62%	£70,000	£43,400
C	£7	£2	£5	71%	£60,000	£42,600

should try either to improve the ratios for A and B or transfer resources from A and B to production of C.

This P/V analysis may be carried out in the following areas:

(a) Product lines as above.

(b) Divisions or factories where the contributions to division or factory sales are calculated.

(c) Salesmen or sales areas.

15. Break-even and budgetary control. The break-even chart
can be applied in the field of budgetary control, *i.e.* the comparison between actual and budgeted sales, costs and profits.
Fig. 54 shows the budgeted total costs and sales and break-even
at 0b or £16,000 sales. However, actual costs are lower than
budget, and since break-even budgeted sales are achieved,
break-even is now at 0a or £14,000 sales. In terms of budgeted
and actual profit the position is as follows:

Budgeted profit = budget sales revenue — budgeted costs
                = £25,000   — £19,000
                = £6,000
Actual profit   = actual sales revenue — actual costs
                = £20,000   — £16,000
                = £4,000
Budgeted profit on actual sales = actual sales — budget costs
                                = £20,000   — £17,000
                                = £3,000
Profit variance = budgeted profit on actual sales — actual
                                                      profit
                = £3,000   — £4,000
                = £1,000 favourable

Managers should explain the cause of this variance, in
particular why sales value is less than target, and why actual
costs are £17,000 and not £16,000 as budgeted for sales of
£20,000.

16. Need for caution. However, the manager is warned that considerable care is required in the interpretation of contribution break-even graphs. It can provide managers with information that if used wisely allows a more flexible approach to

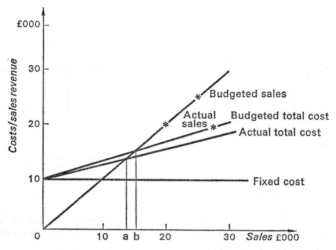

FIG. 54.—Control break-even graph.

decision-making, particularly in the pricing area, but it should not be used independently as an absolute measure. For example, consider Figs. 53 and 55 and the respective contributions of products A and B.

Both Product A and B make a contribution of £21,000 at a level of sales of 7,000. However, further investigation of both charts reveal that product A possesses significant advantages over product B.

(*a*) Product A's profit is £11,000; B's is only £6,000 because the contribution must cover higher fixed cost (£15,000 as opposed to £10,000 for A).

(*b*) Product A's superior profits are confirmed by its broader profit wedge than B's.

(*c*) Product A has a lower break-even level than B. This

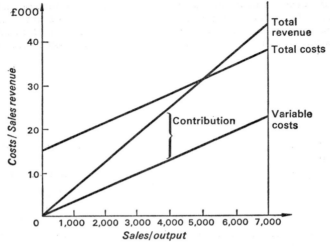

Fig. 55.—Contribution break-even for Product B.

means that if the level of activity is 7,000 units for both products, then sales of A can fall significantly before losses are incurred. This is termed the *margin of safety*.

(*i*) The margin of safety of product A is 3,667 units, £22,002 sales value or 54 per cent.

(*ii*) The margin of safety of product B is 2,000 units, £12,000 sales value or 28 per cent.

17. Financial objectives. Management usually has an idea of a level of profit that provides shareholders with a satisfactory return on their investment. Perhaps in addition they have a profit figure that they hope to earn from the use of all funds employed in the business, whether it is subscribed by shareholders or by finance companies, or banks by way of loans or debentures. Quite clearly it is sensible that they have financial objectives and they are are suitably quantified in order to provide senior and middle management with purpose and direction. Indeed, one could argue that financial objectives are absolutely essential if management is to carry out its duty to protect investors' funds and to make fullest use of their resources. Then with a clearly defined profit target, management can draw up the necessary plans and systems for the motivation and control of staff towards this common end. Furthermore, the achieving of a satisfactory level of profits means that:

(a) Shareholders benefit. A satisfactory level of profits produces immediate benefits in the form of acceptable earnings and dividends, which in the longer term tend to improve the share price.

(b) Management is more likely to use the funds employed in the company efficiently if it achieves a return on capital employed, i.e. $\frac{profits}{capital} \times 100$ that is better than the industry average.

It is difficult to put a figure on a reasonable return on capital employed, for this will depend on the circumstances of the company and trade. Among other things the main considerations determining a reasonable return on capital employed are:

(a) The degree of risk in the trade. For example, companies engaged in oil exploration around the coast of the U.K. face considerable financial risk. In fact it was estimated in 1974 that drilling is twelve times more expensive than, say, in the Middle East. Clearly these oil companies demand, quite reasonably, returns on their investments far in excess of, say, baked beans manufacturers, in order to compensate for the considerably higher risks.

(b) The normal rate of profit for the trade.

(c) The level of dividends that shareholders anticipate, bearing in mind what return they could get elsewhere.

(d) The state of the economy.

(e) The need for profit retention to finance expansion or research and development.

18. Break-even and return on capital. The economist's concept of normal profit is particularly appropriate in the context of break-even and return on capital. It is defined as "the minimum return necessary to keep a factor of production employed in its present occupation." In other words, if management fails to realise the normal profit for the trade, then investors may cut their losses and transfer their funds to more profitable investment elsewhere. In addition, prospective investors will be disinclined to invest in the company.

The economist regards this normal profit as a cost of the business, like the costs of labour, administration, selling and distribution, etc. Clearly, if a company fails to earn sufficient revenue to cover "legitimate" costs of labour, administration and sales, etc., it eventually goes out of business, and just as surely goes out of business if it fails to earn normal profits for the owners.

Economists are quite justified, therefore, in treating this normal profit or satisfactory return for the shareholders as an additional cost. In character it is a fixed cost, and for break-even analysis, added to total costs so that the total cost line is redrawn at a higher level. Fig. 56 assumes a typical cost/revenue/volume relationship. Fixed costs are £50,000 and variable costs are £10 per unit. There are, say, £100,000 worth of shares,

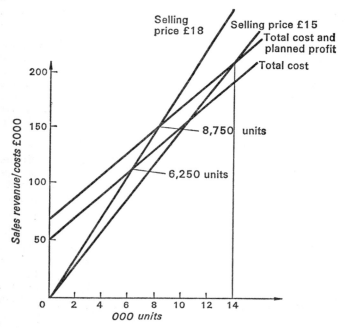

Fig. 56.—Break-even and planned return on capital.

and management calculates that a 20 per cent return (£20,000) before corporation tax will provide shareholders with a satisfactory post-tax return. This means that management must find an additional £20,000 or £70,000 in total to cover fixed costs and to meet their planned profit figure.

19. Break-even and price policy. Fig. 56 is based on an assumption that selling price is initially £15 per unit so that break-even occurs as follows:

(a) 10,000 units if the planned profit figure of £20,000 is ignored.

(b) 14,000 units if these profits are built into overheads.

However, although (b) is conceptually more attractive than (a), it is unsatisfactory in terms of risk because if capacity is 14,000 units then the margin of safety is zero. In other words, the company must sell its entire output to cover costs and meet its profit objective. Failure to match sales and output at the plant's full capacity (which is almost a certainty because of inevitable shortages of materials that occur from time to time, absenteeism and labour turnover, and unplanned bottlenecks in the production process) means that the normal profits of £20,000 are not realised.

The courses of action open to management are as follows:

(a) *To increase selling price.* Consequently, revenue is realised more quickly to cover total costs at a lower level of activity. Diagramatically a new sales revenue line is drawn at a steeper angle so that in Fig. 56 at a selling price of £18, break-even occurs at a level of 8,750 units. Furthermore:

(i) the planned profits are realised;
(ii) the margin of safety is now 5,250 units, or 37·5 per cent of capacity.

Nevertheless, the reader should interpret this information with caution, remembering that it is based on a linear sales revenue line. Only the experience of the sales manager and market research to identify the true demand for the product can tell whether raising the price by £3 and anticipating sales of 8,750 units is a practical proposition.

(b) *To increase plant capacity beyond 14,000 units.* This would improve the margin of safety but at the cost of additional finance for fixed assets and working capital, extra personnel and recording and control systems.

(c) *To reduce variable costs.*

(d) *To reduce fixed costs.* Cost saving in any organisation contributes to profit and in the above situation lowers the total cost line and the break-even point.

20. Cash break-even. Managers, and in particular the management accountant, must always pay close attention to one of its scarcer resources: that of cash. Today, inflation with its attendant high interest rates has increased the cost of cash and made it more important than ever before to control cash effectively. The cash break-even graph can be usefully employed in this respect. The only difference between this graph and the normal break-even graph is in the treatment of fixed costs. They are distinguished as follows:

(a) Costs requiring immediate cash payments are included, *i.e.* administration salaries, rent and rates.

(b) Other costs are ignored for this purpose. These consist of book or non-cash costs, *i.e.*

(i) depreciation charges on assets;

(ii) writing off charges on capitalised research and development expenditure;

(iii) nominal depreciation charges on fully depreciated assets.

Fig. 57 illustrates a typical cash break-even graph.

Fig. 57 shows that at a level of output/sales of OQ, sufficient cash revenue is generated to pay immediate cash expenses.

THE VALUE OF BREAK-EVEN

21. Management planning. This chapter on break-even is not an exhaustive treatment of the subject but serves to provide the manager–reader with an appreciation of the flexibility and scope of this very effective management tool. In particular, a study of break-even analysis, especially from the economist's viewpoint, helps the manager to understand the implications of selected company objectives on costs, revenue and output. A sound grasp is essential. Not only will the

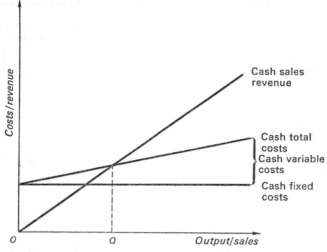

FIG. 57.—Cash break-even graph.

(*i*) Only immediate cash payments are included.
(*ii*) Variable costs are assumed to be for cash. Where credit is taken, such purchases should be eliminated.
(*iii*) Sales revenue is assumed to be for cash. Credit sales should be eliminated.

manager react critically and constructively to objectives proposed for the organisation or department, but when agreed, can plan with greater effectiveness for the attainment of the targets.

In summary, the break-even chart serves as a useful guide to management.

(*a*) It simplifies the relationship between cost, revenue and output which managers must understand for effective performance. This is its most valuable role.

(*b*) It is a useful management planning tool. Provided the underlying assumptions are clearly understood and the limitations appreciated this analysis is useful in the following areas:

(*i*) To calculate the level of sales required to achieve financial objectives.

(*ii*) To determine the selling price that meets the target return on capital.

(*iii*) To calculate the level of activity that achieves break-even in terms of cash transactions, *i.e.* a basis for efficient cash planning.

(*iv*) To compare budgeted and actual sales and costs, *i.e.* as a method of analysing and controlling profit variances.

PROGRESS TEST 12

1. How can break-even analysis be used to illustrate the cost/revenue/volume relationship? **(1–5)**

2. Compare and contrast the economist's and the accountant's view of break-even. **(3–9)**

3. Explain the limitations of straightline break-even analysis. **(11)**

4. Explain the following:

  (*a*) P/V;

  (*b*) contribution break-even;

  (*c*) budgeted total cost;

  (*d*) margin of safety. **(12–16)**

5. Show how the desired return on capital can be incorporated into break-even analysis. **(17–18)**

CHAPTER XIII

PLANNING AND CONTROL BY MEANS OF RATIOS

INTRODUCTION

1. Profitability. Profitability is the relationship between profits and capital and is the most useful indicator of company performance (*see* VIII). At first glance, the term seems unambiguous, but on closer examination there are at least two groups of individuals within the company who view profitability differently.

(*a*) Shareholders are interested in the profits generated by the employment of their funds, *i.e.*

$$\frac{\text{net profits after tax}}{\text{shareholders' capital}} \text{ (Return on investment)}$$

(*b*) Managers are interested in the level of profits generated by the use of total capital, *i.e.*

$$\frac{\text{net profit before tax and interest}}{\text{total capital employed (}i.e.\text{ total assets)}} \begin{array}{l}\text{(return on capital}\\\text{employed)}\end{array}$$

2. Ways to improve profitability. A close examination of the above fractions shows that profitability can be improved by either increasing the numerator (profits) or reducing the denominator (capital). Consequently, management has four variables under its influence or control that directly affect company profitability.

(*a*) *Increase selling price.* If *prices* are raised while costs remain unchanged, or rise by less than the price increase, then the profit margin is increased. However, there is a danger of reaction by customers who may buy cheaper substitutes. It is the elasticity or responsiveness of demand that determines whether sales revenue increases or decreases following a price change. Fig. 58 illustrates the effect of a price increase on sales revenue of a product when demand is

191

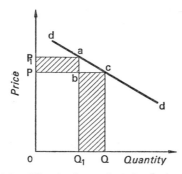

FIG. 58.—Elastic demand and sales revenue.

Initial price OP, initial sales volume OQ.
New price OP₁, new sales revenue OQ₁.
Extra sales revenue PP₁*ab*.
Lost sales revenue Q₁*bc*Q.

elastic (*i.e.* sales volume falls by a larger percentage than the percentage increase in price).

Fig. 59 illustrates inelastic demand. Demand for certain goods (in particular luxuries, necessities and products without substitutes), is unresponsive to changes in price so that sales revenue is increased following price increases. Clearly, elasticity of demand is an important consideration for

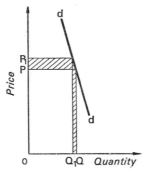

FIG. 59.—Inelastic demand and sales revenue.

government when imposing indirect taxes for additional tax revenue.

(b) *Reduce costs.* The problems and uncertainty of (a) may be overcome by approaching profit from the viewpoint of *costs.* In comparison with selling price, costs are more predictable and under the control of management, so that a more positive way of improving profit margins is to cut costs rather than to increase price. This is clearly seen in the following example:

$$
\begin{array}{ccccc}
\text{Profit per unit} & = & \text{sales price} & - & \text{cost of sales} \\
£10 & = & £100 & - & £90 \\
£15 & = & £100 & - & £85 \\
\end{array}
$$

A comprehensive cost reduction exercise covering the areas of purchasing, production, selling and distribution, administration and research and development could well produce significant savings in costs and consequently a corresponding improvement in profit.

(c) *Increase sales volume.* Increased *sales* on a fixed profit margin improves total profits. However, there are problems associated with an intensive sales drive, particularly in the areas of production, and stock control and working capital.

(d) *Reduce capital employed.* It may be possible to reduce *capital* employed in the business so that sales are maintained from a reduced value of assets. Naturally, this is probably the most difficult of the four methods to effect: a reduction in share capital could be against the interests of creditors, so that a capital reduction scheme requires the confirmation of the courts; a sale and leaseback scheme changes the disposition of assets and not the total amount of capital employed. The obvious answer is to pay off loans and redeem preference shares, and above all, to scrutinise all requests from managers for additional long-term capital to see whether expansion may be financed by better utilisation of existing resources.

3. Profitability ratio. The return on capital employed (R.O.C.E.) shows how efficiently management uses total company funds.

$$
\text{R.O.C.E.} = \frac{\text{profits before tax and interest payments}}{\text{total assets}} \times 100
$$

This is the product of two separate ratios: profit margin and asset turnover.

$$\text{R.O.C.E.} = \frac{\text{profits before tax and interest}}{\text{sales revenue}} \times 100 \times \frac{\text{sales revenue}}{\text{total assets}}$$

i.e.

R.O.C.E. = profit margin   × asset turnover

Thus assuming that sales revenue is £2,000, profits are £100, and that capital employed (or total assets) is £1,000, then the calculations are as follows:

$$\text{R.O.C.E.} = \frac{£100}{£2,000} \times 100 \qquad = 5\% \times \frac{£2,000}{£1,000} = 2$$

R.O.C.E. = 10%

Both profit margin and asset turnover contribute to the R.O.C.E. In retailing, margins are very low, but the very high asset turnover compensates for this and when multiplied together generate a very respectable R.O.C.E. figure. A visit to a supermarket on a Friday evening clearly shows the high asset turnover when whole shelves of goods are sold and replaced several times. On the other hand, capital goods industries, *e.g.* engineering, similarly produce satisfactory R.O.C.E. figures, but through much higher profit margins and lower asset turnover figures. Ideally, managers should understand this relationship and attempt to improve their performance both in the area of profit margins and asset utilisation.

EXAMPLE OF RATIO ANALYSIS. Consider the following information supplied by a small manufacturing company for the year 1972.

	1972
Profit before tax and interest payments	£2,700
Sales revenue	£37,000
Production costs of sales	£27,380
Establishment costs	£1,000
Administration costs	£4,000
General expenses	£1,920
Assets	
Motor van	£1,000
Plant and equipment	£3,000
Land	£10,000
Stock and work in progress	£3,000
Debtors	£4,000
Cash	£1,000
Total	£22,000

This data can now be analysed by means of ratios; there follows a worked example of simple ratio analysis that illustrates the main principles involved in financial control and planning.

$$\text{R.O.C.E.} = \frac{£2,700}{£22,000} \times 100$$
$$= 12 \cdot 2\% \ (7 \cdot 6\%)$$

$$\text{Profit margin} = \frac{£2,700}{£37,000} \times 100$$
$$= 7 \cdot 3\% \ (3 \cdot 8\%)$$

$$\times \ \text{Capital turnover} = \frac{£37,000}{£22,000}$$
$$= 1 \cdot 68 \ (2 \cdot 0)$$

$$\text{Profit} = \text{Sales} - \text{Cost}$$
$$7 \cdot 3\% = 100\% - 92 \cdot 7\% \ (96 \cdot 2\%)$$

Now turn the fraction $\dfrac{\text{sales}}{\text{assets}} \left(\dfrac{£37,000}{£22,000}\right)$ upside down:

Costs and sales percentages

$$\frac{\text{Prod. costs}}{\text{sales}} = \frac{£27,380}{£37,000} \times 100 = 74 \cdot 0\% \ (76 \cdot 6\%)$$

$$\frac{\text{Estab. costs}}{\text{sales}} = \frac{£1,000}{£37,000} \times 100 = 2 \cdot 7\% \ (2 \cdot 6\%)$$

$$\frac{\text{Admin. costs}}{\text{sales}} = \frac{£4,000}{£37,000} \times 100 = 10 \cdot 8\% \ (11 \cdot 9\%)$$

$$\frac{\text{Gen. costs}}{\text{sales}} = \frac{£1,920}{£37,000} \times 100 = \frac{5 \cdot 2\% \ (5 \cdot 1\%)}{92 \cdot 7\% \ (96 \cdot 2\%)}$$

Capital (asset) turnover

$$\frac{\text{M. van}}{\text{sales}} = \frac{£1,000}{£37,000} = 2 \cdot 70\text{p} \ (1 \cdot 00\text{p})$$

$$\frac{\text{plant}}{\text{sales}} = \frac{£3,000}{£37,000} = 8 \cdot 10\text{p} \ (6 \cdot 20\text{p})$$

$$\frac{\text{Land}}{\text{sales}} = \frac{£10,000}{£37,000} = \frac{27 \cdot 02\text{p} \ (25 \cdot 00\text{p})}{37 \cdot 82\text{p} \ (32 \cdot 20\text{p})}$$

$$\frac{\text{stocks}}{\text{sales}} = \frac{£3,000}{£37,000} = 8 \cdot 10\text{p} \ (8 \cdot 00\text{p})$$

$$\frac{\text{drs.}}{\text{sales}} = \frac{£4,000}{£37,000} = 10 \cdot 81\text{p} \ (9 \cdot 75\text{p})$$

$$\frac{\text{cash}}{\text{sales}} = \frac{£1,000}{£37,000} = \frac{2 \cdot 70\text{p} \ (2 \cdot 50\text{p})}{21 \cdot 61\text{p} \ (20 \cdot 25\text{p})}$$

The left-hand side of the example deals with the costs/sales percentages. Since profits are 7·3 per cent of sales, costs must be 92·7 per cent of sales which are further analysed as follows; production costs 74 per cent, establishment 2·7 per cent, administration 10·8 per cent and general costs 5·2 per cent.

The right-hand side deals with capital or asset turnover. However for convenience, the fraction $\dfrac{\text{sales revenue}}{\text{total assets}}$ is reversed so that $\dfrac{\text{motor van}}{\text{sales}} = 2 \cdot 7$ which means that 2·7p worth of investment in a motor van is required to generate one pound of sales revenue. Similarly 8·1p of plant, 27·02p of land and in total 35·66p of fixed assets is needed to produce a pound's worth of sales revenue. The corresponding figure for total current assets is 21·61p.

However, the corresponding ratios for 1973 (figures in brackets) reveal that the R.O.C.E. is down to 7·6 per cent (the product of a lower profit margin of 3·8 per cent and a slightly higher asset turnover of 2·0), and clearly show the usefulness of ratios as a control technique. Obviously higher costs have caused the deterioration in the profit margin. In particular, the ratio of production costs/sales has increased from 74 per cent to 76·6 per cent, so that if we assume that the 1972 ratios are the norm or standard for the organisation, management should immediately examine the production area to establish the reason for the unfavourable variance of 2·6 per cent. This may reveal the following:

			1972	1973
$\dfrac{\text{production costs}}{\text{sales revenue}}$	×	100	74%	76·6%
$\dfrac{\text{labour costs}}{\text{sales revenue}}$	×	100	36·6%	37·7%
$\dfrac{\text{material costs}}{\text{sales revenue}}$	×	100	37·4%	38·9%

The explanation may lie in higher wage rates or overtime workings and higher prices of materials, which if controllable, demand immediate remedial action in the areas of work schedules to avoid costly overtime payments, and in the buying department to obtain cheaper supplies.

Similarly, the higher administration costs should be investigated. Fortunately, small economies in establishment costs and general costs partly offset the diseconomies within production and administration.

The right-hand side of the figure reveals a more efficient use of both fixed and current assets in 1973. Asset turnover is higher so that in total, 52·45p of assets are needed to produce £1 of sales revenue compared with 59·43p in 1972. Dealing firstly with fixed assets, we see that a smaller value of motor vans is required to support the sales revenue (1·00p compared with 2·7p in 1972) and relatively less capital per £1 of sales revenue is tied up in plant and land, *i.e.* 6·20p and 25·00p respectively. Furthermore, less money is tied up in all current assets so that only 20·25p is required in 1973 (21·61p in 1972).

4. Advantages of ratio analysis. The advantages of ratio analysis are as follows:

(*a*) The system requires a thorough examination of all activities, which provides senior managers and staff with a surer understanding of the nature of activities and their inter-relationships.

(b) It helps to identify defects or weaknesses in the system.

(c) It provides a basis for setting target objectives for managers and assessing managers' performance.

(d) It provides managers with information about their departments, which is comprehensible and of use in controlling their activities. It must be emphasised how important it is for managers:

(i) to understand the need for ratios and

(ii) the relationship between them;

(iii) to be actively involved in the drawing-up of standard ratios for their departments;

(iv) to monitor and compare their performance and progress by means of ratios;

(v) to take prompt remedial action when variances occur.

(e) The R.O.C.E. is important in planning. Ideally, the R.O.C.E. is a threshold return and only those projects realising the R.O.C.E. figure should be considered, and that with the highest return selected for implementation. Obviously a new project that fails to make the present R.O.C.E. figure must lower the overall R.O.C.E. for the organisation. A project that beats the R.O.C.E. figure naturally improves overall profitability.

(f) Inter-firm comparisons tell managers how successful they are, compared with similar companies in the same industry.

GEARING

5. Capital gearing. The gearing ratio, or coefficient, indicates the relative proportions of the types of capital employed in a company. For example, a company is said to be *highly geared* if the proportion of fixed income capital is large in relation to the total. The gearing ratio can be measured by:

(a) the proportion of total debt interest and preference share dividends to total ordinary share dividends;

   (b) the coefficient,

$$\frac{\text{long-term debt} + \text{preference share capital}}{\text{ordinary share capital} + \text{reserves}}$$

   (c) the percentage,

$$\frac{\text{total borrowings}}{\text{equity}}$$

6. Determinants of the gearing ratio. The ratio varies between firms and industries and is influenced by the following factors:

   (a) The borrowing powers in a company's Articles of Association.

   (b) The existence of charges on the company's assets.

   (c) The attitude of shareholders towards control. They may resist attempts to diffuse their equity holding, and prefer *debt* capital as a source of new finance.

   (d) The relative costs of raising debt and share capital.

   (e) The level of anticipated profits in relation to the fixed interest charges on debt capital.

7. Effect of gearing on profits. A simple example illustrates the effect of different gearing ratios on company dividends. Let us assume there are two equally capitalised companies but with different capital structures: A is low-geared (1:4) and B is high-geared (7:3). Company A has a share capital of 20,000 at £1, preference at 5 per cent, 80,000 ordinary at £1. Company B has a share capital of 70,000 £1, preference at 5 per cent, 30,000 ordinary £1. Profits in each case for 1971, 1972 and 1973 are £9,000, £7,000 and £4,000 respectively.

TABLE XIII.—EFFECT OF GEARING RATIOS ON COMPANY PROFITS.

Company	1971 A	1971 B	1972 A	1972 B	1973 A	1973 B
Total profits for distribution:	£9,000		£7,000		£4,000	
Total dividends for 5 per cent preference shares:	1,000	3,500	1,000	3,500	1,000	3,500
Dividends for ordinary shares:	8,000	5,500	6,000	3,500	3,000	500
Dividend percentage:	10	18·3	7·5	11·6	3·7	1·6

   Thus, if one ignores taxation and profit retention, one sees that the high gearing in Company B produces higher dividends at higher profits and lower dividends at lower profit levels, in contrast to Company A. This has important implications for companies and shareholders.

8. Effect of gearing on profitability. It is quite possible for a company earning only a modest R.O.C.E. to produce attractive returns on the shareholders' equity by means of gearing. For example, if the R.O.C.E. figure is, say, 10 per cent, but half of the assets are financed by debenture, loan stock and preference shares, then the return on net worth (ordinary shareholders' funds) is as follows:

$$\text{Return on net worth} = \frac{\text{R.O.C.E.}}{\text{Percentage of assets financed by net worth}}$$

$$= \frac{10\%}{50\%}$$

$$= 20\%$$

Naturally there is a limit to which a company can use gearing to boost returns on net worth. Creditors may become reluctant to advance additional loans on the grounds that they and not the shareholders are bearing the risk; shareholders may also feel that risk of bankruptcy which would result from a default or debt interest payment becomes unacceptable at higher levels of gearing.

9. Advantages of gearing.

(*a*) When profits are high in relation to total fixed interest charges, the ordinary shareholders in a highly geared company benefit immediately from additional dividends, or in the future from the earnings generated by the retained profits.

(*b*) Gearing enables a company to increase its capital without dilution of equity and shareholders' control.

10. Disadvantages of gearing.

(*a*) High gearing is disadvantageous to equity holders when profits are falling, since they receive disproportionately less by way of dividends.

(*b*) The company is committed to long-term fixed interest payments.

(*c*) If gearing is affected by debentures, then charges may be placed on company assets.

(*d*) Once assets are pledged, further gearing may be accomplished only by offering higher yields to lenders to compensate for the lack of security.

(e) Gearing demands that management produce sufficient profits to pay interests and dividends and meanwhile establish a sinking fund for the redemption of debentures.

(f) Companies whose incomes fluctuate (perhaps their products are elastic in demand) will find it difficult to maintain satisfactory dividend rates and share prices.

(g) Investors will be reluctant to subscribe new capital.

PROGRESS TEST 13

1. How can a firm improve its R.O.C.E.? (1–2)
2. Identify the advantages of ratio analysis. (3–4)
3. Explain how gearing can influence profitability. (7–10)

CHAPTER XIV

INVESTMENT APPRAISAL

INTRODUCTION

1. The nature of investment. In VI we looked at the "water tank analogy" which introduced the concept of *investment appraisal*. There, managers were faced with the problem of how to use company money, *i.e.* choosing between the many competing uses for the company's limited financial resources. The decision was made by a process of *investment appraisal* so far undefined.

Investment in this context may be defined generally as "the commitment of company resources in the expectation that it will realise a profit or gain." Usually it means capital expenditure on fixed assets, although it should include leasing agreements, which commits current and future expenditure for the use (if not ownership) of assets. Clearly these investment decisions must not be made lightly but only after rigorous appraisal of the alternative project, because such investment once made is often irreversible and thus commits management to a fixed policy in the future. Furthermore it introduces risk since the anticipated profit or gain cannot be guaranteed at the outset. In summary the nature of company investment is such that:

(*a*) a decision is often irreversible since abandonment would probably involve considerable financial loss if the asset were resold;

(*b*) it introduces inflexibility into future company policy;

(*c*) it means that the expenditure is at risk because future incomes cannot be forecast exactly.

With the greater cost-consciousness on the part of management, and increasing capital intensiveness in industry, it is vital that managers pay more and more attention to the various techniques of capital appraisal to secure the optimum use of company and departmental resources. The principal investment appraisal techniques available to managers are now considered in detail.

2. The need for preparatory work. Before we can undertake any application of investment appraisal technique it is vital to assemble data that is accurate. In particular we need to know:

(*a*) The capital cost of the project and its operational life, additional working capital required, and any scrap value at the end.

(*b*) A forecast of additional net revenue arising from the project (*i.e.* sales revenue − operating costs).

(*c*) The tax liability of earnings and any tax savings for which the investment may qualify.

These estimates are fundamental to meaningful investment analysis, so that it is imperative to guarantee accuracy of information. Therefore maximum time and effort should be expended on estimation and data collection, for the quality of information determines the quality of the investment decision and unquestionably decisions based on faulty data could prove to be very expensive mistakes.

METHODS OF MEASURING THE PROFITABILITY OF CAPITAL PROJECTS

3. Accounting rate of return method. This measures the return on an investment as a percentage of the capital expenditure.

$$\% \text{ rate of return} = \frac{\text{total revenue} - \text{total operating costs} \times 100}{\text{capital expenditure}}$$
$$or \quad \frac{\text{net earnings}}{\text{investment}} \times 100$$

Assume that a company buys an automatic press for £12,000 which is expected to have an operational life of six years, at which time it will have no scrap value. Gross earnings arise by way of savings in wages and present operating costs, and are expected to amount to about £2,500 per year. The calculations involved in this example are as follows:

TABLE XIV.—CALCULATION FOR THE PROFITABILITY OF A
CAPITAL PROJECT.

Year	Gross earnings (i)	Depreciation (ii) (straight line)	Net earnings (i — ii)
1	£2,500	£2,000	£500
2	2,500	2,000	500
3	2,500	2,000	500
4	2,500	2,000	500
5	2,500	2,000	500
6	2,500	2,000	500
	£15,000	£12,000	£3,000

Here, gross earnings (ignoring taxation) are increased by
£2,500 per year by the reduction in labour and operational
costs, or £500 per year *after* charging depreciation on a straight
line method over its operational life. Thus we are attempting
to remove the replacement part of the cash flow, and calculate
the true profit element of cash flow in relation to the cost of
the project. Thus:

$$\frac{\text{net earnings}}{\text{investment}} \times 100 = \frac{£3,000}{£12,000} \times 100$$
$$= 25\% \ (or \ 25\text{p per £1 of investment})$$

The return measured on a yearly basis is:

$$\frac{£500}{£12,000} \times 100$$
$$= 4 \cdot 16\% \text{ per annum}$$

If the company had a choice of several automatic presses,
all of which would perform satisfactorily, then we should
calculate the profitability of each and seriously consider the
one showing the highest percentage rate of return. However,
because of the disadvantages of this method (*see* **4**), it is
dangerous to use it for making investment decisions, but rather
as a guide to performance of alternative investments.

4. Disadvantages of the method. The disadvantages of the
rate of return (or yield) method are as follows:

(*a*) It fails to take time into account, weighting each £

equally. Thus it disregards the incidence of cash flows. However, £1 received in Year 1 is obviously worth more than £1 in Years 2, 3, 4, 5 and 6, since it can be invested immediately to earn interest. Similarly, money received in Years 3, 4, 5 and 6 is worth less than money received in Years 1 and 2.

(b) Bearing in mind the limitations experienced in (a), it will be misleading to compare two projects which have different earning profiles, i.e. income accrues at different times over the operational life of each project.

	Project A *Alpha Automatic Press* *net earnings*	Project B *Beta Automatic Press* *net earnings*
Year 1	£1,000	£2,000
Year 2	1,000	2,000
Year 3	1,500	1,000
Year 4	2,000	500
	£5,500	£5,500

The accounting rate of return method will give identical answers for both machines if their capital costs are identical, but project B may be preferred on the grounds that the bulk of the net earnings is received in the very early years.

Throughout this example we have ignored taxation and thus the return is gross. However, taxation may be taken into account and the net return calculated by deducting tax from the net earnings and adding savings through capital allowances to the net taxed earnings.

5. Advantages of the method.

(a) It is simple to understand and calculate.

(b) It gives an indication of overall profitability since it measures savings over the entire life of the project and relates it to the investment.

6. Payback method. This method measures the length of time it takes to recoup the capital outlay out of the expected earnings. Earnings here is usually defined as pre-tax profit plus depreciation. It is a simple concept to operate and can be illustrated by way of example.

Assume that a company is about to launch a new product which is thought by the marketing manager to have a reasonably long product life cycle. He illustrates this by means of a diagram:

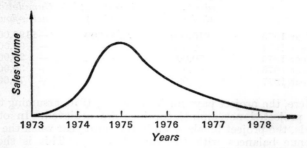

FIG. 60.—Product life cycle of "Swallow" brand cassette tape-recorder.

The marketing manager explains this typical product life cycle curve as follows:

1973   Period of production innovation when sales increase slowly. Development and launching costs are being incurred so that profits are low.

1974   Period of maximum growth in sales. The public quickly appreciate the novelty of the product and a high sales volume generates high profits.

1975   Period of maturity of the product. In a competitive market, rivals are launching similar goods which slows down the growth in sales. Higher marketing costs to counteract rival products tend to reduce profits.

1976   Period of decline. Profits fall rapidly as customers prefer competitors' products as they are newer and probably incorporate technological improvements.

NOTE: In 1964/5, 96 per cent of companies used payback gross of tax (A. J. Merrett and A. Sykes).

EXAMPLE. Payback: in the light of the Swallow brand's product life cycle, let us imagine that the initial capital outlay (Column ii) on manufacturing equipment is £200,000, and net profits from sales are as shown in column i:

	i Net annual earnings (inflow)	ii Investment (outflow)	iii Cumulative net inflow
Year 1973	£10,000	£200,000	−£190,000
Year 1974	100,000	—	− 90,000
Year 1975	70,000	—	− 20,000
Year 1976	50,000	—	+ 30,000
Year 1977	40,000	—	+ 70,000

Here, the project pays for itself during 1976, assuming that the projected net annual earnings are achieved. In other words, the project breaks even in the third year when the net revenue balances with the capital outlay. This is shown graphically in Fig. 61.

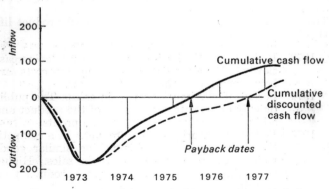

FIG. 61.—Payback method of investment appraisal.

7. Advantages of the payback method. The main advantages of this method are:

(a) It is simple to calculate.
(b) It recognises the timing of cash flow.

(c) It is particularly appropriate and informative for a company short of liquid assets. In this case then, only projects with short payback periods are likely to be selected.

(d) It is valuable as a method for investment decisions for a company in a changing market. Companies whose products tend to be overtaken by changing technology or fashion and therefore have short product life cycles, will prefer short payback periods.

8. Disadvantages of the payback method. The chief disadvantages are:

(a) It ignores the value of receipts after the point of recovery of original capital outlay.

(b) It fails to consider the timing of receipts beyond the break-even point.

(c) It ignores the profitability of the project, since it is preoccupied with speed of repayment.

(d) If the company is concerned with liquidity then payback measured gross of tax understates the true cash flow and is therefore inaccurate.

9. Compound interest. The investment appraisal methods that we next consider have one thing in common. They are all based on the concept of *present value, i.e.* they overcome the objections raised against payback and accounting rate of return by considering the time value of money, which means additional weight is given to immediate cash flows than to future cash flows. To appreciate the real significance of this concept, let us look firstly at compound interest.

If an investor deposits £100 in a deposit account of a bank that pays 10 per cent interest then the total investment will grow as follows:

	Initial deposit	Interest 10%	Total deposit
At start of Year 1	£100	—	£100·00
At end of Year 1	—	£10·00	£110·00
At end of Year 2	—	£11·00	£121·00
At end of Year 3	—	£12·10	£133·10
At end of Year 4	—	£13·31	£146·41

A visual presentation may help the reader to appreciate the effect of compound interest:

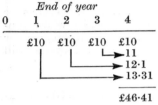

	End of year			
0	1	2	3	4
	£10	£10	£10	£10

£46·41   Total interest received on invest-
―――――   ment of £100 in Year 1.

Of course it is possible to use a formula to calculate these totals. The formula for calculating compound interest is $(1 + i)^n$ where i is the rate of interest and n is the number of years that the principal sum is invested.

Thus to calculate the interest that £1 will earn at 10 per cent over four years so as to check the above table, we substitute the values of i and n in the formula.

$$
\begin{aligned}
\text{Compound interest} &= (1 + i)^n \\
&= (1 + \cdot 10)^4 \\
&= 1\cdot1 \times 1\cdot1 \times 1\cdot1 \times 1\cdot1 \\
&= 1\cdot461
\end{aligned}
$$

If we extend the formula to include the initial sum invested (*principal*) then the total sum invested at the end of a period is calculated by the formula: $P(1 + i)^n$.

$$
\begin{aligned}
&= £100 \, (1 + i)^n \\
&= £146\cdot41 \quad \text{This is the sum invested at the end of fourth year.}
\end{aligned}
$$

At the outset it is important to appreciate the following:

(*a*) £1 now is worth more than £1 in the future because the present £1 can be invested and will in time be equal to £1 plus interest.

(*b*) This analysis does not consider the depreciation in the value of future money caused by inflation, *e.g.* the purchasing power of the pound taken as 100p in 1970 was equivalent to 85½p in 1972. However, inflation may be taken into account indirectly because interest rates (and therefore interest receipts on investments) tend to increase in periods of inflation. Thus we are concerned only with the effect of interest payments on money invested.

10. Discounting. Discounting is compound interest in reverse. It tells us the present value of a future sum of money. For example if an investor wants exactly £100 at the end of year one when the rate of interest is 10 per cent, then he must invest £90.91 now.

The reader is probably wondering where this figure of £90.91 come from. The answer is simple. We know that £100 with interest of 10 per cent will grow to £110 at the end of one year. If we divide:

£100 by £110 then we obtain 0·9091 for year one, and
£100 by £121 then we obtain 0·8264 for year two.

These figures are called *discount factors* and inform us that:

£1·00 at the end of one year is worth £0·9091 *now* at 10 per cent, and
£1·00 at the end of two years is worth £0·8264 *now* at 10 per cent.

Using these factors we can reduce any sum of money back to present-day value. For example:

$$0·9091 \times £110 = £100·00$$
$$0·8264 \times £121 = £100·00$$

Returning to a visual presentation, if £100 is received at the end of each year for four years, then in present value terms the total cash flow is worth £316·98.

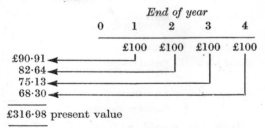

	End of year			
0	1	2	3	4
	£100	£100	£100	£100

£90·91
82·64
75·13
68·30

£316·98 present value

A short formula for calculating the discount factor is $\dfrac{1}{(1 + i)^n}$, so that we can substitute the information for year one in this example in the formula:

$$\frac{1}{(1 + \cdot 10)^1_i} = \frac{1}{11} = 0\cdot 9091$$

£1 at the end of year one is worth £0·9091 now. The investor is indifferent between receiving £0·9091 immediately or £1·00 at the end of one year.

EXAMPLE: Examine this example carefully, and complete the calculations of the discount factors using the formula $\frac{1}{(1 + i)^n}$ Indicate exactly how much must be invested at the outset to achieve precisely £100 at the end of years 1, 2, 3 and 4.

	Compound Interest			Present Values	
	deposit	interest	total deposit	discount factor	present value of £100
Year 0 100	—	£100		
Year 1 (end) —	£10	£110	$\frac{1}{(1 + 0\cdot10)^1}$ $= 0\cdot9091$	$0\cdot9091 \times £100$ $= £90\cdot91$
2 (end) —	£11	£121	$\frac{1}{(1 + 0\cdot10)^2}$ $= 0\cdot8264$	$0\cdot8264 \times £100$ $= £82\cdot64$
3 (end) —	£12·10	£133·10	=	=
4 (end) —	£13·21	£146·41	=	=

11. What the discount rate means. Let us assume that Ivor Hogg borrows £200 from a building society at 11 per cent, and repays the loan over two years. The transactions are as follows:

		i	ii
		£200	
Start of year 1	Capital outstanding	200	
	Interest on this capital (11%)	22	
		222	11% discount factor
End of year 1	Repayments	117	× 0·9009 = £105·4
Start of year 2	Capital outstanding	105	
	Interest on this capital (11%)	12	
		117	
End of year 2	Repayments	117	× 0·8116 = £94·9
	Capital outstanding	—	£200·00

Ivor has repaid a total of £117 + £117 = £234. This represents a repayment of the loan of £200 plus interest payments of 11 per cent which is the true annual rate of interest on the capital outstanding on the loan. Column ii confirms that the repayments repay the £200 capital when brought back to present values.

12. Discounting problem. Ivor Hogg's godmother offers him as a token of affection a present of £1,000 in cash immediately, or a larger sum of £1,100 at the end of three years when Ivor will certainly need the money for school fees for his child. Ivor recognises that the larger sum will offset the effects of inflation, and seriously considers accepting the promise of £1,100 in three years time. Advise Ivor which he should accept on the basis that interest rates will remain at 8 per cent over the period, using both compounding and discounting methods (*see* **9, 10**).

13. Present value tables. If one is to have a sound grasp of the concept of discounting, it is critical to understand the meaning of discount rates and how the discount factors are determined. Indeed this was the purpose behind **12, 13, 14** and **15**. However, this chore is unnecessary in practice because present value tables are readily available in most management accounting and budgeting books.

14. Present value of future earnings. So far we have applied discounting to investment income resulting from a deposit of money at compound interest, but in fact it has a far wider application. If we now reconsider the financial data set out in the table below we can apply this discounting technique to future earnings arising from a company's investment that are unlike bank deposit interest in that they are positively skewed as reflected by the product life-cycle diagram. By assuming that the project is expected to achieve a 10 per cent return we discount future earnings at 10 per cent and thereby give greater weighting to earnings achieved in the immediate periods. This is demonstrated by a new break-even point: payback is now put back one year and occurs during 1977.

15. Definition of discounted cash flow method. The discounted cash flow (D.C.F.) rate of return on an investment is defined as the annual return on the outstanding capital balance at the end of each year. This rate of discount makes the present-day value of future cash flow equal in aggregate the present-day capital cost of the project.

TABLE XV.—APPLICATION OF THE DISCOUNTING TECHNIQUE
TO FUTURE EARNINGS.

	Net annual earnings	Discount factor (10%)	Discounted net annual earnings	Cumulative net inflow (discounted)
Year 1973	£10,000	0·9091	£9,090	−£190,910
Year 1974	100,000	0·8264	£82,640	−£108,270
Year 1975	70,000	0·7513	£52,590	− £55,680
Year 1976	50,000	0·6830	£34,150	− £21,530
Year 1977	40,000	0·6209	£24,830	+ £3,300
			£203,300	

16. Discounted Cash Flow (D.C.F.). Now that we have
defined the D.C.F. rate of return we can illustrate its operation
by using the estimated annual sales, costs and capital outlay
of the Swallow brand cassette recorder set out on p. 206. In
15 we discounted the net earnings at 10 per cent. This produced total net earnings measured at present day values of
£203,300 which exceeded the present-day value of the cost of
the project (£200,000) by £3,300. Therefore a 10 per cent discount factor is too low; the return must be greater than 10
per cent.

Let us now discount the earnings at the higher rate of 11 per
cent.

In comparison with the previous calculation, this calculation
produces a negative balance of £1,990 and shows that an 11
per cent discount rate is too high so that the true rate lies

TABLE XVI.—APPLICATION OF THE DISCOUNTING TECHNIQUE
TO FUTURE EARNINGS AT A HIGHER RATE.

Year	Net annual earnings	Discount factor 11%	Discounted net earnings
1973	£10,000	0·9009	9,000
1974	100,000	0·8116	81,160
1975	70,000	0·7312	51,180
1976	50,000	0·6587	32,930
1977	40,000	0·5935	23,740
			£198,010

between 10 per cent and 11 per cent where the discounted cash flow exactly equals the cost of the investment. In summary:

(a) The D.C.F. is too high if present value of future earnings is less than the cost of the investment.

(b) The D.C.F. rate is too low if the present value of future earnings is more than the cost of the investment.

(c) The true D.C.F. rate is that when present value of future earnings equals the cost of the investment.

17. D.C.F. rate by interpolation. This method shown in **16** is appropriately known as the *trial and error* method, since at least two calculations must be made that straddle the true rate. This rate is then found by interpolation.

Net present value of earnings at 10% = + £3,300
Net present value of earnings at 11% = − £1,990

Overall difference $\qquad$ £5,290

Therefore the true discount is found by interpolation; it lies at a point $\dfrac{3,300}{5,290}$ of the difference between 10 and 11 per cent, *i.e.* 10 per cent + 0·62 per cent or, 10·62 per cent.

Thus the profits from the project are sufficient to repay the cost of the investment and earn a rate of interest on the capital of 10·62 per cent per annum.

18. Net present value method. This method also makes use of discount factors. When this method is used for investment decision, the cash flows are discounted at a stipulated rate of discount to give their present-day values. A company faced with a choice between two competing projects should select the one showing the largest surplus of earnings at present-day values. An example serves to illustrate this technique.

Assume that a company can borrow sufficient funds at 10 per cent to finance one of two projects it has under considera-tion. The minimum acceptable return on capital for the com-pany is 12 per cent. This difference of 2 per cent represents the return to compensate for the risk inherent in the project. The capital expenditure required for projects A and B is £25,000 and net cash flow can be seen in the table.

The calculation shows that both projects achieve a return in

TABLE XVII.—NET CASH FLOW FOR PROJECTS A AND B.

Net cash flow	PROJECT A	PROJECT B
Year 1973	£7,000	£12,000
Year 1974	£12,000	£10,000
Year 1975	£15,000	£8,000
Total net cash flow	£34,000	£30,000

Calculations of NPV (net present values) at discount rate of 10 per cent p.a.

	PROJECT A			PROJECT B		
	Net cash flow	*Discount factor*	*Discounted net present value*	*Net cash flow*	*Discount factor*	*Discounted net present value*
Year 1973	£7,000	0·9091	£6,363	£12,000	0·9091	£10,909
Year 1974	£12,000	0·8264	£9,916	£10,000	0·8264	£8,264
Year 1975	£15,000	0·7513	£11,269	£8,000	0·7513	£6,010
	£34,000		£27,548	£30,000		£25,183
	Less : Capital cost		25,000	*Less :* Capital cost		25,000
	NPV =		2,548	NPV =		183

Calculations of net present values at discount rate of 12 per cent p.a.

Year 1973	£7,000	0·8929	£6,250	£12,000	0·8929	£10,714
Year 1974	£12,000	0·7972	£9,566	£10,000	0·7972	£7,972
Year 1975	£15,000	0·7118	£10,677	£8,000	0·7118	£5,694
	£34,000		£26,493	£30,000		£24,380
	Less : Capital cost		25,000	*Less :* Capital cost		25,000
	NPV =		1,493	NPV =		(620)

excess of the 10 per cent, the cost of capital, but only project
A passes the threshold return of 12 per cent and is therefore
preferable to B.

19. The choice of discount rate.

(*a*) The stipulated rate of interest may be the organisation's
R.O.C.E. percentage. Possible projects that fail to meet this
test should be disregarded, projects whose profitability exceeds
this figure will tend to improve the organisation's overall
profitability.

(*b*) It may be the company's cost of capital. For example, if
the capital structure of the company is:

$$\begin{array}{llll}
\text{Ordinary shares:} & \text{£100,000:} & \text{dividend } 11\% = & \text{£11,000} \\
\text{Debenture} & \underline{\text{£50,000}} & \text{interest } \quad 8\% = & \underline{\text{£4,000}} \\
& \text{£150,000} & : & \text{£15,000}
\end{array}$$

$$Average\ cost\ of\ capital = \frac{£15,000}{£150,000}$$
$$= 10\%$$

Here the cost of servicing the capital is 10 per cent and any new project should at least cover these costs by earning 10 per cent or more.

(c) It may be based on the cost of capital plus a percentage for uncertainty or the degree of risk.

(d) Certain projects or capital expenditure produce a nil return as, for example, expenditure on safety installations. Nevertheless, they cannot be rejected merely on profitability grounds.

20. Ranking investment proposals. At this stage the reader should have a clear idea of the various investment decision techniques that are currently used. Certainly the manager who bids for additional capital resources and who submits details of costs, projected earnings or cost savings will better understand the purpose behind such requests for information and how the final decision may be made.

A company possessing limited resources and faced with several projects each competing for funds may select projects by ranking them in order of:

(a) Payback.
(b) Accounting rate of return.
(c) Net present value.
(d) Profitability index, which is the net present value of net earnings divided by the present value of the capital outlay.

Thus at 10 per cent discount rate the profitability indices for projects A and B described in **18** are:

$$\frac{\text{Net present earnings}}{\text{Capital outlay}} \quad \overset{A}{\frac{£27,548}{£25,000}} = 1 \cdot 101 : \overset{B}{\frac{£25,183}{£25,000}} = 1 \cdot 007$$

This confirms our conclusions reached in **18** that at a 10 per cent discount rate both projects succeed, but if they are mutually exclusive then A is preferred to B on the basis of its higher profitability index number.

21. Ranking projects and D.C.F. The observant reader will have noticed that the D.C.F. method did not appear above as a means of ranking investment projects. This is because, unlike the other methods, it fails to take into account the cost of the capital expenditure. However, this is not a serious obstacle and in view of D.C.F.'s significant overall advantages (*see* **22**) should not appear to be deficient in this respect. Consequently a ranking procedure for D.C.F. follows:

Assume that management has two alternative projects under consideration. A requires a capital outlay of £120,000, but B needs £180,000. Both are estimated to provide a cash flow for five years; A £40,000 per year and B £58,000 per year. The capital can be borrowed by debenture at 10 per cent per annum.

TABLE XVIII.—CALCULATION OF DISCOUNTED CASH FLOW
FOR PROJECTS A AND B.

		PROJECT A			PROJECT B	
	Net earnings	Discount 10%	Discounted net earnings	Net earnings	Discount 10%	Discounted net earnings
Year 1	£40,000	0·9090	£36,360	£58,000	0·9090	£52,722
Year 2	40,000	0·8265	33,060	58,000	0·8265	47,937
Year 3	40,000	0·7513	30,052	58,000	0·7513	43,575
Year 4	40,000	0·6830	27,320	58,000	0·6830	39,614
Year 5	40,000	0·6209	24,836	58,000	0·6209	36,012
			151,628			219,860
	Less : Capital outlay		120,000	Less : Capital outlay		180,000
		NPV	£31,628		NPV	£39,860
	By trial and error Yield = 19·8%			Yield = 18·5%		

The calculation shows that project A is preferable in that it earns a higher D.C.F. rate, but it must be remembered that each requires different capital investments. Thus we are not comparing like with like.

However, we may usefully employ the economist's concept of the margin, and by comparing the two projects, calculate the marginal or incremental capital outlay and marginal net earnings.

	Capital outlay	*Annual net earnings*
A	£120,000	£40,000
B	£180,000	£58,000
Marginal investment =	£ 60,000	Marginal earnings = £18,000
		Yield = 15·7%

Thus the marginal capital of £60,000 invested in project B generates marginal earnings of £18,000 per annum which earns a D.C.F. rate of 15·7 per cent.

To conclude, the second project ranks on par with project A, but the incremental investment of £60,000 generates additional earnings that yield 15·7 per cent which is to be preferred, bearing in mind that the cost of the capital is only 10 per cent.

22. Advantages of D.C.F. rate. The D.C.F. rate has certain advantages over other capital appraisal techniques:

(*a*) It is expressed as a percentage.

(*b*) As a percentage it is easily understood by managers who conventionally measure profitability and yields in this way.

(*c*) It can be readily compared with the cost of capital which is also expressed as a percentage.

EXAMPLES OF APPLICATION OF D.C.F.

23. Determination of annual rentals. Goggle Box Services Limited wish to rent out a black and white TV set to a new customer. Their policy is to charge an annual rental that within four years pays for the set (£300) and in addition generates a 15 per cent return. The rental is determined as follows (ignore tax and capital allowances):

Year	Discount factor 15%
0	1·0000
1	0·8695
2	0·7561
3	0·6575
	3·2831 *total factors*

$$\frac{\text{capital investment}}{\text{total factors}} = \text{rental/year}$$

$$\frac{£300}{3·2831} = £91·37 \text{ p.a.}$$

24. Lease or buy. The owner-manager of the Wayside Garage is interested in installing a diagnostic-tuning system and establishes that such a machine can be bought for £4,000, or rented for £600 per annum. In both cases, operating costs and maintenance are borne by the garage. The anticipated life of the equipment is ten years. Obviously the running costs and sales revenue are identical whether the equipment is bought or leased so the decision rests on the relative capital costs of acquiring the system. The garage at present earns 16 per cent return on capital.

Cost of purchase	*Cost of rental*
Cost = £4,000	Rent cost £600 p.a.
Present value = £4,000	Present value of £1 for 10 years at 16% = 4·833
	Present value of £600 = 4·833 × £600
	Rent = £2,899

Therefore on these comparative costs the rental agreement is preferable as it produces the lower present value.

NOTE: In this example the rental agreement requires the garage to pay a regular fixed sum of £600 per annum for ten years (which is like an annuity). We could employ the same method as in **23**, but this would be tedious considering the life of the project. Fortunately there is a short cut. We look therefore in a compound interest table called *Present value of an annuity of £1* for the appropriate term (ten years) and at the appropriate rate of interest, in this case 16 per cent (4·833).

25. D.C.F. and non-monetary considerations. The following example typifies the problems that many organisations faced prior to conversion to decimalisation in 1971. Costs alone do not always determine the outcome of an investment decision, but an attempt should always be made to quantify the relative costs so that judgments can be made based on facts.

EXAMPLE. Superstores established a new branch in Bucks. in 1969 and required certain capital equipment, among which were ten cash registers. The manager was faced with a choice of *either* xx machines for £650 each which in 1971 would need converting to decimalisation for £100 each, *or* xx+ machines for £735 which were dual currency and therefore required no conversion. The test rate of discount for the organisation was 12 per cent.

xx Machines		
1969 Capital outlay £650 × 10	=	£6,500
1971 Conversion £100 × 10 = £1,000		
P.V. of £1,000:		
£1,000 × 12% discount factor in year 2 = £1,000 × 0.7972	=	797
Total present value	=	£7,297

xx+ Machines	
1969 present value £735 × 10 =	£7,350
	£7,350

Clearly the xx machines were cheaper in 1969 present value terms. However, the manager decided to purchase the more expensive xx+ machines, on the grounds that the machine suppliers would be inundated with similar demands for conversion on D. Day − 1. Failure to convert would mean at the most closure and lost sales revenue or at the least, additional expenses on buying suitable replacement machines. In other words, the security of having dual currency machines outweighed the cost advantages of the xx cash registers.

26. Optimum time to replace a car. Let us attempt to calculate the ideal time to replace a car. We are able to get an idea of the resale value of a car over a number of years by reference to *Motorist Guide*, etc. This might reveal that a saloon car costing £1,977 new would resell for the values shown in Column *i* below.

TABLE XIX.—CALCULATION OF OPTIMUM TIME FOR THE REPLACEMENT OF A CAR.

	i	*ii*	*iii*	*iv*	*v*	*vi*	*vii*	*viii*	*ix*
Year	*Resale value*	*Capital cost*	*Running costs*	*10% factors*	*Running costs (disc.)*	*Total running costs (disc.)*	*Total cap. costs (disc.)*	*Total costs (disc.)*	*Average costs*
1	£1,740	£237	£10	0·9091	9	9	215	224	224
2	1,460	517	40	0·8264	33	42	427	469	234
3	1,210	767	70	0·7513	52	94	576	670	223
4	1,005	972	120	0·6830	81	175	663	838	209
5	820	1,157	100	0·6209	62	237	718	955	191
6	685	1,292	80	0·5644	45	282	729	1,011	168
7	555	1,422	100	0·5131	51	333	729	1,062	151

Notes: Col. *ii* Difference between new price £1,977 and resale values.
iii Assumed exceptional expenses per year, *e.g.* repairs, new tyres, etc.
iv 10 per cent is assumed throughout.
v Col. *iii* × Col. *iv*.
vii Col. *ii* × Col. *iv*.
viii Col. *vi* + *vii*.
ix Col. *viii* ÷ appropriate year.

If the car is replaced at the end of the first year, then the total costs incurred are the capital cost and the running costs for that year, *i.e.* £224.

However, if it is replaced at the end of the second year then the capital cost is incurred (£517) and the running costs for year 1 and 2 (£50). When discounted they represent £469, or an average of £234 per year.

Thus costs are minimised by replacing the car at the end of year one; to do so at year 2 would prove more costly. Alternatively, one should drive the car into the ground which would be even more economical. Costs per year are only £151 at present values if it is replaced at year 7.

Fleet users, car rental companies and large-scale users of vehicles will in fact do similar calculations to establish when they should replace vehicles. In fact, their replacement policy tends to be very accurate because the exact pattern of repairs —and there are no exceptional running expenses—is quickly established when many vehicles are operated. Furthermore, their costings take into account the various tax allowances allowed to owners of the vehicles. In the above example, taxation allowances have been ignored for the sake of simplicity but if they were to be included, then they would reduce the annual capital cost, and therefore the annual total costs, according to the amount and timing of the allowances.

27. Accuracy of estimates. The prerequisites for accurate investment appraisal are:

(*a*) Correct forecasts of capital:

    (*i*) Capital expenditure required.
    (*ii*) The life of the project.
    (*iii*) Working capital required.
    (*iv*) Residual value of the equipment.
    (*v*) Tax rates and allowances.

(*b*) Correct forecasts of net revenue generated by the investment:

    (*i*) The selling price of the article.
    (*ii*) The volume of sales.
    (*iii*) The operating costs.

28. Errors in estimates. It is obvious that in reality the forecasts are unlikely to be perfectly accurate. To offset these errors it is common practice to prepare estimates of cash flow at these levels:

    (a) Most favourable.
    (b) Least favourable.
    (c) Most likely.

Thus if the forecasts of profits from the sale of cassette recorders as set out in **7** are thought to be realistic in that they are based on the most accurate costing and sales figures, then we can regard the figures as the most likely to occur. However, we may estimate that there is a likely range within which actual profits may fall. The most optimistic level of profits may lie 5 per cent above the expected level; the most pessimistic level may lie, say, 10 per cent below the most likely level.

The profits or cash flows can then be calculated for these two extreme levels, and D.C.F. or *net present values* calculated to see in particular whether the most pessimistic level meets the investment criterion. If the minimum acceptable return

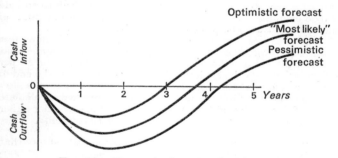

FIG. 62.—Forecast of expected cash flows.

for the organisation is 10 per cent and the return at the least favourable level is, say, 8 per cent, then the capital may be invested elsewhere for higher returns at less risk. If, however, it suggests a minimum return of 12 per cent then the project is viable since it satisfies the minimum return requirement and stands a very high chance of exceeding this most pessimistic figure. Figure 62 illustrates the three assumptions of expected cash flows.

29. Discounting methods and taxation. In order to assess the precise return on an investment it is necessary to consider the post-tax earnings generated by the project. However, we have disregarded taxation so far to facilitate an appreciation of the basic principles of this fairly complex subject: this over-simplification can now be remedied. The basic rules for dealing with taxation are as follows:

(a) The net earnings before depreciation arising from the capital outlay should be adjusted for corporation tax liability.

(b) Any investment allowances on the profit should be calculated, and the savings in corporation tax set off against company tax liability.

EXAMPLE. An example will illustrate the effect of taxation on cash flow. However, it should be remembered that taxation rates and methods of providing capital allowances are changed by the annual *Finance Acts*, and that consequently it is difficult to provide a single example that describes the tax situation at one point in time. Nevertheless the principles are clear.

Let us re-examine the effect of taxation and capital allowances on the two projects A and B (*see* p. 204). If we assume that both cost £3,000 and qualify for a capital allowance of 25 per cent per annum on the capital balances outstanding at the end of each year, and that the organisation earns sufficient profits else-where to utilise the full taxation allowances, then we can calculate the cash flows generated by both projects and see whether either one or both satisfy a cut off rate of return of 10 per cent.

The table below summarises the calculations and shows that for project A in year 1, since no tax is paid, cash flow is £1,300; £1,000 plus £300 tax savings which may be offset against company profits in that year to reduce the tax bill. However, in year 5 £800 tax is paid on the profits of year 4 so that a cash out-flow occurs. Project B is treated in an identical way. Thus the present values of the cash flows for projects A and B are £3,360 and £3,572 respectively, showing that both satisfy the 10 per cent rate of return, but that B earns a higher return (after tax) than A and is therefore preferred.

TABLE XX.—SUMMARY OF CALCULATIONS FOR PROJECTS A AND B.

PROJECT A

i	ii	iii	iv	v	vi	vii	viii	ix
Year	Capital outlay	Capital allowance	Earnings gross of tax	Corporation tax 40%	Tax savings	Cash flow	Present value factors for 10%	Present value
1	£3,000	£750	£1,000	—	£300	£1,300	0·9090	£1,181
2	2,250	562	1,000	£400	224	824	0·8264	681
3	1,688	422	1,500	400	168	1,268	0·7513	952
4	1,266	316	2,000	600	126	1,526	0·6830	1,042
5	—	—	—	800	—	(800)	0·6209	(496)
								3,360

PROJECT B

1	3,000	750	2,000	—	300	2,300	0·9090	2,090
2	2,250	562	2,000	800	224	1,424	0·8264	1,176
3	1,688	422	1,000	800	168	368	0·7513	276
4	1,266	316	500	400	126	226	0·6830	154
5	—	—	—	200	—	(200)	0·6209	(124)
								3,572

Explanation of columns

i and iv — Data supplied by **4** (b).
ii and iii — 25 per cent capital allowance on capital outstanding each year.
v — Corporation tax payable on gross earnings and in arrears of one year.
vi — Tax savings are 40 per cent of the capital allowance for each year.
vii — Cash flow represents the gross earnings (iv) *less* the tax paid in that year (v) *plus* the tax savings for that year (vi).
viii — The assumed rate of discount is 10 per cent.
ix — The present value is the cash flow discounted at 10 per cent (vii × viii).

PROGRESS TEST 14

1. How do investment proposals arise? (1–2)
2. Discuss the pros and cons of payback and the accounting rate of return method in investment appraisal. (3–8)
3. Explain the following terms:

(a) D.C.F.;

(*b*) N.P.V.;
(*c*) Trial and error;
(*d*) Profitability index. (**10–29**)

APPENDIX I

BIBLIOGRAPHY

BUSINESS MANAGEMENT

Ansoff, H. I., *Business Strategy: selected readings* (Penguin).
Ansoff, H. I., *Corporate Strategy* (McGraw-Hill).
Chamberlain, N. W., *The Firm: micro and economic planning and action* (McGraw-Hill).
Dean, J., *Managerial Economics* (Prentice-Hall).
Humble, J. W., *Improving Business Results* (McGraw-Hill).
Koontz, J. and O'Donnell, C. J., *Principles of Management* (McGraw-Hill).
Presanis, A., *Corporate Planning in Industry* (Business Publications).
Pugh, D. S., Hickson, D. J. and Hinings, C. R., *Writers on Organisations* (Penguin).
Savage, C. I. and Small, J. R., *Introduction to Managerial Economics* (Hutchinson).
Speight, H., *Economics and Industrial Efficiency* (Macmillan).
Wood, J. C. (ed.), *Cooper's Outlines of Industrial Law* (Butterworths).

FINANCIAL MANAGEMENT

Amey, L. R., *The Efficiency of Business Enterprises* (Allen & Unwin).
A.C.C.A., *A Quotation for your Shares* (A.C.C.A.).
A.C.C.A., *Sources of Capital* (A.C.C.A.).
Carsberg, B. V. and Edey, H. C. (eds.), *Modern Financial Management: selected readings* (Penguin).
Chambers, R. J., *Financial Management* (Sweet & Maxwell).
Clarkson, C. P. E. and Elliott, B. J., *Managing Money and Finance* (Gower Press).
de Paula, F. C., *Management Accounting in Practice* (Pitman).
Hunt, P., Williams, C. M. and Donaldson, G., *Basic Business Finance: text and cases* (Irwin).
I.C.M.A., *The Profitable Use of Capital in Industry* (I.C.M.A.).
Jackson, A. S. and Townsend, E. C., *Financial Management* (Harrap).
Merrett, A. J. and Sykes, A., *The Finance and Analysis of Capital Projects* (Longmans).
Moon, R. W., *Business Mergers and Take-over Bids* (Gee).

225

Page, C. S. and Canaway, E. E., *Finance for Management* (Heinemann).

Paish, F. W., *Business Finance* (Pitman).

Palmer, R. E. and Taylor, A. H., *Financial Planning and Control* (Pan).

Samuels, J. M. and Wilkes, F. M., *Management for Company Finance* (Nelson).

Solomon, E. (ed.), *The Management of Corporate Capital* (Collier-Macmillan).

Solomons, D., *Divisional Performance: measurement and control* (Financial Executives Research Foundation).

Van Horne, J. C., *Financial Management and Policy* (Prentice-Hall).

Wright, M. G., *Discounted Cash Flow* (McGraw-Hill).

Wright, M. G., *Financial Management* (McGraw-Hill).

Key to Abbreviations:

A.C.C.A.   Association of Certified Accountants.

I.C.M.A.   Institute of Cost and Management Accountants.

EXAMINATION TECHNIQUE

Examination questions may be classified as follows:

(a) Text-book questions which test your memory of your text books and your ability to marshal and organise information. For example, "Explain the following terms in relation to invest-ment: (i) P/E ratio; (ii) Earnings yield, etc."

(b) Applied questions which test your knowledge and your ability to apply it to the facts in the question or which test your appreciation of current financial problems and policies. For example, "Compare and contrast bank overdrafts and bank loans as sources of working capital for the small firm."

Procedure at the examination.

(a) Read all the questions to get the "feel" of the examination paper and to establish precisely what is required.

(b) Select the questions which you feel you can answer best, bearing in mind your knowledge and ability. Your choice may be limited, as when questions have to be selected from sections within the paper; e.g. "Answer five questions only: one question must be taken from each part and the fifth question may be taken from any part." Any such instructions must be followed.

(c) Allocate equal time to each question or apportion time according to the marks carried by each question where indicated. Remember that "diminishing returns" apply to examination answers; it is comparatively easy to get pass marks but a dis-proportionate amount of time has to be put in to get very high marks.

(d) Think about each question, jot down the relevant points as they come to mind and shuffle them into a tidy legible plan on the answer paper. Delete it only when you have completed the answer.

(e) Write legibly.

(f) Write your answers in essay form unless you are asked to list points or write a report or letter. Write your answer in short concise sentences without slang or unacceptable abbreviations and try to start paragraphs with "key sentences." Finally, check your answer through for inaccuracies.

(g) Do not be politically biased in your answer, and do not

waste time attempting to sway the examiner by humour or appeals.

(*h*) Do not give cross references between questions; *e.g.* "I have already explained this in my answer to question 3."

(*i*) You are attempting to impress the examiner and should appear widely read, so give frequent examples. Also, answers may be improved by the use of economic concepts; *e.g.* elasticity and long- and short-run comparisons.

(*j*) Do not panic.

EXAMINATION QUESTIONS

1. What is "investment?" Discuss the effects on an economy of an increase in investment.

2. Assess the effect of a rise in the minimum lending rate on:

(a) Gilt-edge prices.
(b) Equity prices.

3. Explain what is meant by "capital gearing" and "vote gearing." Assess the effect of corporation tax on capital gearing in large British companies.

4. Discuss the advantages and disadvantages of a "Rights Issue" from the following viewpoints:

(a) The company.
(b) The shareholder.

5. Discuss the considerations which tend to determine the purchase price of a business.

6. Outline the main features of convertible loan stock and explain why they have appeared in recent years.

7. "Monetary and fiscal policies must be complementary for effective economic management." Comment.

8. Describe in detail the ways in which British banks help to finance trade.

9. Distinguish clearly between the following:

(a) Private placing of shares.
(b) Stock exchange introduction.
(c) Stock exchange placing.

10. What is a Bonus Issue? Discuss the desirability or otherwise of such an issue from the point of view of (a) the company; (b) the shareholder.

11. Write notes on the following:

(a) Barter.
(b) Banks reserve ratio.
(c) The capital market.
(d) Cash flow.
(e) Responsibility accounting.

12. Compare and contrast fiscal and monetary policy as investments of government economic policy.

13. Describe the activities of Issuing Houses.

14. Write notes on the following:

    (*a*) Prospectus.
    (*b*) Underwriting.
    (*c*) Sale and leaseback.
    (*d*) Trade credit.
    (*e*) The "cost of credit."
    (*f*) "Specialised finance."

15. Outline the duties and responsibilities of accountants.

16. (*a*) What is meant by "depreciation?"
    (*b*) Describe two methods of providing for depreciation.

17. Explain these costs:

    (*a*) Fixed.
    (*b*) Variable.
    (*c*) Marginal.
    (*d*) Sunk.
    (*e*) Opportunity.

18. Describe three costing systems.

19. Distinguish carefully between capital and revenue expenditure.

20. Describe the contents of a typical balance sheet. What would a bank manager look for in the company's Profit and Loss Account and Balance Sheet when considering a request for extra overdraft facilities?

21. Explain the structure and value of a funds flow statement.

22. Distinguish between margin and mark-up.

23. Write notes on the following:

    (*a*) Gearing.
    (*b*) R.O.C.E.
    (*c*) E.P.S.
    (*d*) Solvency.
    (*e*) Asset turnover.

24. Define a "budget" and the purpose of a budgetary control system.

25. Write notes on the following:

    (*a*) Cost centres.
    (*b*) Corporate objectives.
    (*c*) Cash forecast.
    (*d*) Master budget.
    (*e*) Variances.
    (*f*) Management by exception.

26. "Marginal costing and contribution analysis are extremely useful tools for management in decision making and cost control." Discuss.

27. Explain with examples, five applications of marginal analysis.

28. Describe in detail three methods of investment appraisal generally used in industry.

29. Write notes on the following terms commonly used in investment appraisal.

    (a) D.C.F.
    (b) N.P.V.
    (c) Payback.

30. "The D.C.F. rate is too high if the present value of future earnings is less than the cost of the original investment." Discuss.

31. Explain the nature and value of break-even analysis.

GLOSSARY OF FINANCIAL TERMS

accounts payable: company creditors.

accounts receivable: company debtors.

acid test: see the *quick ratio.*

allocation of overheads: the charging of the whole overhead to the appropriate cost centre or unit incurring the expense.

apportioning of overheads: where overheads cannot be allocated they are apportioned or shared by cost centres or units on an equitable basis.

Articles of Association: the internal rules and regulations of a company that stipulate the rights and duties of shareholders and directors and procedures for meetings.

assets: expenditure to acquire a long- or short-term item of value as opposed to expenditure incurred in the process of earning income; anything of value held by a business.

asset turnover: the ratio of sales to assets, *i.e.* the number of times that assets are utilised in a year.

bear: an investor who believes that prices of securities will fall.

blue chip: an ordinary share of highest investment status.

bonus issue: the free issue of shares to existing ordinary shareholders on a proportionate basis, paid for out of the built-up undistributed profits of the business.

book value: the value of an asset as shown in the Balance Sheet; usually cost less total depreciation to date.

break-up value/ordinary share: the residual value of net assets accruing to each ordinary share if the company went into liquidation.

bull: an investor who believes that the price of securities will rise.

capital employed: the total of the shareholders' funds, loan capital and any other long-term sources of funds; generally, intangible and fictitious assets, are excluded.

capital reserve: a reserve that does not arise from retention of trading profits, *e.g.* share premium, capital redemption reserve fund. Since the 1967 Companies Act, Balance Sheets need not distinguish between capital and revenue reserves.

cash flow: retained profit plus depreciation.

circulating assets: "current assets," the most liquid of assets that will be converted into cash within the short term, *e.g.* stocks, debtors.

close company: a company controlled by five or fewer shareholders.

collateral security: any security offered in support of a debt.

consolidated Balance Sheet: the Balance Sheet showing the financial state of affairs of a group of companies.

contingent liabilities: a possible liability rather than one of a definite nature, shown as a note to the Balance Sheet, *e.g.* the contingent liability arising from a contract agreed but not yet executed.

convertible loan stock: loan stock that may be converted into ordinary shares at predetermined time and price.

cost unit: a cost unit of quantity of output or service.

coupon: the stated rate of interest on a loan security.

cumulative preference shares: preference shares where any arrears of dividend are paid prior to other shareholders.

current assets: assets of a short-term nature that change from day-to-day, being part of the cycle leading to cash, *e.g.* stock, debtors, cash.

current liabilities: the claims that must be paid within the short term, *e.g.* dividends and tax payable and creditors.

current ratio: a measure of liquidity, *i.e.* current assets to current liabilities. A test of liquidity: 2 is the general norm.

current taxation: company corporation tax that is to be paid within the year.

current yield: the dividend expressed as a percentage of the current price of the security.

debenture: a certificate issued under seal by a company acknowledging a debt.

deferred liabilities: a subdivision of long-term liabilities, *e.g.* tax payable next year and not of a fund-raising nature such as debentures.

deferred taxation: corporation tax payable by a company in the longer term, *i.e.* not within one year.

depreciation: the reduction in value of an asset due to obsolescence, wear and tear or the passing of time.

directors' emoluments: payments to directors for services in this capacity.

discounted cash flow: the present value of future cash inflows and outflows.

dividend: profits paid to shareholders expressed as a percentage of the nominal value of their shares.

dividend cover: earnings per share divided by dividend per share, *i.e.* the number of times that earnings cover the declared dividend.

dividend yield: see *current yield.*

earnings per share: the post-tax profits figures available for the ordinary shareholders divided by the number of shares.

earnings yield: this measures how much an investor could get at current earnings if he invested £100 in the company's shares at their current price, *i.e.* earnings per share divided by current market price.

equity: see *net worth.*

fictitious assets: these items appear on the Balance Sheet because they have not been written-off against the profits of the business, *e.g.* long-term advertising expenditure, which is written-off over the expected period of benefit from the expenditure.

first in first out (*F.I.F.O.*): a basis for costing the material content of a job on the basis the oldest stocks are used first.

fixed assets: assets of a long-term nature held for the purpose of earning profits, *e.g.* machinery, land and buildings. The nature of the business determines whether an asset in a particular case is fixed or current, *e.g.* normally a motor vehicle would be a fixed asset, whereas in a vehicle-selling firm, the vehicles held at any one time would be more of the nature of stock and are, therefore, current assets.

fixed overheads: expenses that do not vary with output.

free depreciation: whereby a company can write-off the cost of fixed assets how it wishes.

funds statement: "flow of funds statement" or "sources and uses of funds statement" that shows the sources of new funds and the uses to which they are put.

gearing: the relationship between the loan capital, preference capital and ordinary capital of a business. A high-geared company is one where the prior charges, *i.e.* loan and preference capital, are high in relation to the ordinary capital. The reverse is described as low-geared.

goodwill: the net value of a business after the deduction of tangible assets; also the excess of the purchase price over the value of the net assets of a purchased company. (An intangible asset.)

historical cost: the original cost of assets.

holding company: a company that owns the share capital of other companies.

insolvency: inability to meet debts.

intangible assets: an intangible asset is not physical, yet has long-term value to the business, *e.g.* goodwill, patent, trademarks.

introduction: a method of issuing shares onto the stock exchange.

inventory: stocks in hand.

job cost: a cost unit consisting of a single job or contract.

K: = kilo = 1,000.

last in first out: (*L.I.F.O.*): a basis for costing the material content of a job on the basis that the newest stocks are used first.

leverage: see *gearing.*

liabilities: amounts that a business owes to shareholders and outsiders. These may include debts of either a short-term or long-term nature.

limited liability company: a company limited by shares or guarantee is one where members are responsible only to the extent of their share capital or guarantee in the event of liquidation.

liquid assets: current assets minus stocks, being the least liquid current asset.

long-term liabilities: long-term debts as opposed to capital, *e.g.* debenture or loan stock.

marginal cost: the cost of producing one extra unit = variable cost.

marginal revenue: the revenue from one extra sale.

margin of safety: the excess of sales over the break-even volume.

market value of a share: the market value has no meaning in Balance Sheet terms, merely representing the price which a share will realise if sold at any particular point in time.

Memorandum of Association: the constitution of the company, enabling outsiders to assess its structure and powers.

minority interests: these represent the capital and built-up reserves of a group of companies owned by shareholders outside the group.

net assets: the total of the fixed and current assets less the current liabilities of the business.

net current assets: see *working capital.*

net worth: the "equity" of a business representing the total ordinary share capital made up of paid-up ordinary share capital and reserves owned by the ordinary shareholders.

ordinary shareholders funds: the total of issued ordinary share capital plus the total of the revenue and capital reserves.

ordinary shares: that part of the share capital subscribed for by shareholders not entitled to a fixed rate of dividend and not entitled to any preference for repayment of capital in the event of the winding-up of the company.

paid-up capital: a "fully-paid" share is one where the nominal value has been fully subscribed; whereas a share of, say, nominal value of £1, if only 50p has been subscribed per share, is described as "partly paid."

par value: when issued "at par" the issue price is equal to the nominal value. When issued at a "premium" the issue price is in excess of the nominal value, and when at a "discount," below the nominal value.

ploughed-back profits: profits retained in the business.

preference shares: that part of the share capital preferred to the remainder of the ordinary share capital for the payment of dividend and/or for the repayment of capital on a winding-up.

price earnings (P/E): current market price of the share dividend by the last reported earnings attributable to the share.

prime costs: the total of direct materials, labour and expenses.

private company: a company whose Articles of Association restrict the transfer of its shares, limit its members to fifty and prohibit public advertisements for capital.

profit volume ratio (P/V): the rate at which profits change with a change in output.

provision: a charge against profit that provides for the reduction in value of an asset or a liability whose value is uncertain, *e.g.* provision for depreciation, provision for doubtful debt.

public company: a company that is not a private company.

quick assets: see *liquid assets*.

quick ratio: the ratio of liquid assets to current liabilities. A test of liquidity: 1 is the general norm.

reserves: these represent the build-up of undistributed profits and consist either of revenue or of capital reserves.

retained profits: see *ploughed-back profits*.

revenue reserves: these are distributable as dividend to the shareholders whereas capital reserves may only be distributed to shareholders in a restricted manner, *i.e.* basically by the issue of fully-paid bonus shares.

rights issue: an issue of shares for cash to existing holders of share capital in the company. Normally the issue is at a price lower than the current market price, acting as an inducement to existing holders to take up the shares.

share capital: the amount raised from the shareholders of the business.

shareholders' funds: the total of ordinary and preference issued capital plus the total of the revenue and capital reserves.

share premium: a capital reserve owned by the shareholders arising when a company issues shares at a price in excess of the nominal value.

source and uses of funds: see *funds statement*.

standard cost: a predetermined cost, *i.e.* what it ought to cost to produce something.

standard hour: a hypothetical hour that measures the amount of work that ought to be carried out in the hour.

stock turnover: ratio of cost of sales to stocks. This measures the number of times stocks are turned over in the course of a year.

tangible asset: a physical asset.

times interest earned: the number of times that loan interest is covered by profits, *i.e.* earnings (profits) before tax and interest divided by the interest charge. It indicates how safe creditors interest charges are.

trading as the equity: whereby a company takes advantage of high gearing, paying a modest fixed interest charge for funds that are employed to earn a higher return for the ordinary shareholders.

turnover (assets): the number of times that total assets are turned over to generate sales revenue, *i.e.* the ratio of sales to assets.

turnover (sales): the total value of sales.

variable overheads: indirect expenses that vary directly with output *e.g.* power.

variances: the difference between a budgeted performance and the actual performance achieved.

wasting assets: assets of a fixed nature but as they are being used by the business are physically diminishing in size, *e.g.* a mine.

working capital: the total of the current assets less the current liabilities.

work in progress: semi-finished goods.

yield: the rate of return on an investment.

INDEX